Second Edition

Don & Carol Raycraft

ISBN 0-87069-302-6
Library of Congress Catalog
Card No. 77-0726

Published By

Wallace-Homestead Book Co.
1912 Grand Avenue
Des Moines, IA 50305

Contents

Acknowledgments

The following individuals contributed time, talent, or information to the development of this book. Their skills, collections, and advice were invaluable to the project.

Dr. David D. Darnall
Elmer and Marilyn Fedder
Linda Valine Hay
Judge Sam Harrod III
Mike and Martha Hilliard
Gordon and Jean Ann Honegger
Captain Alex Hood
Alex Moonan
J. Maxwell and Opal Pickens
Mel and Kay Schultz
Dale and Vonnie Troyer
Larry and Kathy Troyer
Lloyd Troyer
Delmar and Judy Valine

Photography

Ron Hayes and Bruce Benedict
Mel Schultz
Dave Bertsche
Barb Bertsche
Elmer Fedder
Mike Hilliard
Linda Thornton
Barry Spitznass
A. I. Weintraub

Lighting

Craig, Scott, and Mike Raycraft

Preface

Attempting to place values on American country antiques is, at best, a questionable and presumptuous occupation. To use the results of auctions as the sole indicator of the price trends in the field often borders in the realm of questionable sanity. There is a rare tropical disease that inhabits auction houses in New York City or backyard sales in Watseka, Illinois. It matters not whether it is a warm spring day or a rainy morning in October. The psychology of the situation is interesting because a person can, by merely scratching his nose or occasionally raising his fist, hold an audience of eleven or eleven hundred in awe of his ability to spend money with untempered ease. This moment in the sunlight is worth a great deal to many people. By purchasing large quantities of Fiesta Ware at the closing-out sale on the corner or weathervanes at Sotheby Parke Bernet, an indiviual may recapture the same positive reinforcement that Dan Reed's uncle always savored when people asked, "Who was that masked man?"

The almost audible buzz and cloud of mystery that envelopes the person who pays a seemingly outrageous sum for a particular object is probably reward enough for most masked people.

A classic example occurred at the auction of the Stewart Gregory Folk Art Collection at Sotheby Parke Bernet in New York City in January, 1979. The presale catalog of the collection estimated a "carved and painted wood barn ornament, American, 19th century, carved in the form of a five-pointed star, the center with louvered slats. Painted green. Diameter 37 inches" to be worth somewhere between $300 and $500.

The vast majority of the readers of this publication would question the heredity of a dealer who priced a similar barn accouterment at $400 ($300 and $500 divided by two) in a shop or at a show. The presale estimate probably was also considered a bit high by most students of the catalog because the star was certainly not one of the major pieces of the collection.

The *Newtown* (Conn.) *Bee* reported that Mr. Gregory had paid approximately $75 for the star. It is important to keep in mind that what an individual pays for a particular object has little relevance to what it is sold for a week or twenty years later. It is possible, though not highly probable, that it may be worth considerably less down the road of time than it is today. Tastes change and objects considered to be of significant merit today may emerge in the future to a less than appreciative audience of buyers who have gone off in totally different directions. A classic example of this are paintings by particular artists whose works sold for thousands in the 1920s but mere hundreds in the 1980s.

Sotheby Park Bernet tacks on a 10 percent charge to the final bid that is paid by the buyer for the pleasure of doing business with such an established firm. The purchaser of the "carved and painted barn ornament" paid Sotheby Park Bernet $375 and Mr. Gregory's estate $3,750.

Auction fever like the disco and baseball varieties do exist. The symptoms of ego involvement, frustration, anger, and hostility are identical at the closing out farm sale in Iowa or the Gregory auction in New York. Perceived values and desires get caught up in a complex emotional entanglement and often prices are paid and purchases made that the buyer cannot believe when the fever subsides.

1 Price Guides and Buying Antiques

The majority of the price guides to antiques that we have read provide lengthy lists of prices. It appears to us that with glass, stamps, coins, or autographs it is possible to successfully inform readers in this manner. There are very few pieces of country furniture that can be adequately described without an illustration. There is no standard piece of stoneware, woodenware, or furniture. Antiques are a visual experience and pictures provide a measure of comparison with examples the collector may own or may have recently had the opportunity to purchase.

The purpose of any price guide is to offer the reader some insights into approximate or "ballpark" values. It is impossible to provide definitive values or prices because they do not exist. Value is determined only by what one individual will sell an item for and by what another will pay at that particular time.

For readers who are conditioned to lists of prices we have carefully chosen twenty-seven offerings from shows, shops, and auctions in 1980 that were of interest to us. It would be possible to provide an almost endless list, but it would serve no purpose.

Twenty-Seven Country Items Offered for Sale in 1980

Trestle table, 7′ long, Maine, possibly Shaker, $3,000, New Hampshire auction.

Decorated dome-top immigrant chest, dated 1818, $400.

Dry sink, small drawer upper left, open well, three-door cupboard base, old finish, $395, New Jersey dealer.

Blanket chest, early one drawer, high bootjack sides, original red, New Jersey dealer, $395.

Cupboard, two 2-panel doors, pegged solid sides, cutout base, gallery, good red paint, $410, New Jersey dealer.

Shoe foot chair table, blue paint, $1,600, Massachusetts auction.

Pie safe, twelve punched tins, drawer above, $785, Pennsylvania dealer.

Damaged apothecary chest, missing seven and a half of the thirty-six drawers, some old paint remaining, $650, New Hampshire auction.

Mount Lebanon Shaker #6 chair, original finish, taped back and seat, $275, Michigan dealer.

Pine dovetailed cradle, original red paint, Lancaster County, Pennsylvania, $295, Pennsylvania dealer.

Walnut two-drawer farm table, pinned top, Hepplewhite legs, $595, Pennsylvania dealer.

Six-drawer miniature walnut chest, Chippendale style, c. 1810, $295, Pennsylvania dealer.

Set of four decorated chairs, rabbit ears, $1,200, New Hampshire auction.

Breadboard and matching bread knife, $125, Canadian show.

Three graduated pantry boxes, blue-green paint, $105, New Hampshire dealer.

Pie lifter, hand wrought tines, wooden handle, $40, New Hampshire dealer.

Small candle box, original black and brown paint, slide top, 7″ high x 3″ wide x 3¼″ deep, $35, Massachusetts dealer.

Noah's Ark with sixteen animals and four people, c. 1890, $75, Ontario show.

Mid-eighteenth century leather shoes, American, worn condition, $85, New Hampshire dealer.

Brass barber's basin, $240, Maryland dealer.

Rockingham milk pan, 10¼″ high, $85, New Hampshire dealer.

C. Crolius, New York jug, minor repair to lip, $215, North Carolina dealer.

Crock, 1½ gallon, blue decoration, signed Solomon Bell, Strasburg, Virginia, $175, Virginia dealer.

Stoneware, twenty-three heavily decorated pieces, offered for $60,000 at New York City show.

The collector of country antiques is facing a rapidly increasing number of rivals and a diminishing supply of early furniture, pottery, lighting, and kitchenware. The authors have had the best experience in finding early things at the shops of specific dealers who specialize in quality early Americana. Antiques may also be found at shows, auctions, flea markets, and private homes.

Periodically in most sections of the country associations of antiques dealers or private individuals rent an auditorium or use shopping center malls for shows and sales. The dealers who rent space are much more interested in the sale aspect than in the showing of antiques.

The primary advantage of antiques shows for the collector is the instant insight into the relative values of pieces that are available. Sales and shows may be utilized as a price guide to the collector's own early furniture, lighting, pottery, and kitchen related antiques. Dealers are usually limited in the amount of furniture they can transport to the show and many often bring only smaller pieces. We have had several opportunities to purchase large case pieces (cupboards, desks) at reduced prices in the final hours of the final day of antiques shows. It is often easier for the dealer to sell a piece at or near his cost than to haul it home.

In recent years costs for dealers have skyrocketed to the point that they are often very selective in the shows they do. Booth rental, gasoline, food, lodging, and the cost of acquiring merchandise have taken much of the profit out of the antiques business and forced retail prices even higher.

It appears to us that as the energy crunch gets tighter and tighter and lengthy buying trips are curtailed, quality shows will become increasingly more important for collectors. A problem is that collectors of New England and country antiques, Victoriana, and glassware attend shows where a literal smorgasbord of merchandise is presented. Items may range from African tribal art to depression glass to stoneware pottery. Thus in a show with 150 dealers offering their wares only 20 to 30 may exhibit the specific type of items that a collector is interested in purchasing.

There is a trend in some areas to produce shows that are limited in the type of merchandise that is allowed to be sold. For example, a spring and fall show may feature dealers who stock only country related antiques and a winter and summer show may offer glass or advertising.

By limiting the number of shows and carefully choosing dealers with representative items it is possible to produce a word of mouth mystique that draws people from a wide geographic area. In July, 1979, we attended a one day outdoor show in Dorset, Vermont, that was outstanding. The dealers from New York and New England offered a wide variety of early things in a beautiful and relaxed setting. It is our understanding that it is held every other year and provides collectors with the opportunity to save their money for two years while salivating with anticipation.

Another gradually growing trend at some shows is to allow collectors willing to pay a premium ($20-$50) the opportunity to get into a show an hour or two before the official opening and make purchases.

The flea market phenomenum has swept the country in recent years. A flea market is a sale of short duration where a large number of collectors, junk dealers, housewives who have cleaned out their attics, and part-time antiques dealers come together to buy, sell, and trade. A major center for weekend flea markets is just off the Pennsylvania Turnpike near Adamstown. The Black Angus, Renningers, and Shupps Grove offer an opportunity to see an awful lot of stuff in a limited amount of time. We have bought a few early things and have seen many late things in these markets. It is essential that the collector arrive with the first wave of dealers to capture anything of merit. As the vans and trucks are being unloaded in the moonlight the best purchases are usually made.

The value of attending auctions is distinctly related to the area of the country in which the collector lives. A country auction in New England, New York, Pennsylvania, or Ohio always offers the chance for a number of early family pieces to quietly emerge. A farm auction in central Illinois generally consists of a houseful of oak from Sears and Roebuck. The country pine that preceded the mass-produced oak was given to the hired man or burned when the new furniture arrived.

The finest auctions for collectors to attend are probably those held by fellow collectors disposing of their antiques. The popular belief of antiques dealers dominating any auction by their presence and checkbooks is false. The dealers must purchase a piece at a price that covers their expenses and an additional 15 percent to 50 percent for profit.

Many times the "buy" of the day at most auctions turns out to be a piece of homemade cherry pie for thirty cents.

2 Notes on Becoming a National Authority

In times of economic flux when the price of gold and silver rises to a point that brings out the grave robbers and a 1964 dime is worth an eight-pack of Pepsi plus the deposit, many people suddenly get interested in antiques. We have not provided the following information for collectors of napkin rings, barbed wire, valentines, golden oak, or telephone pole insulators. The terms are aimed primarily at individuals who can't sleep the night before an auction of country furniture or a major antiques show. The minds of these people are not filled with fantasies of Bo Derek or Robert Redford but with visions of cheese baskets, bird jugs, sugar plums, and painted cupboards.

We have put together a list of twenty-five crucial "buzz" words with which accumulators of early Americana need to be conversant and five sentences they need to repress.

The following five statements are *worse* than using faulty subject-verb agreement or triple negatives. These are equally as important to learn to avoid as the buzz words are to learn to use.

"We threw out a whole attic full."

"I don't know how to describe it, but I will know it when I see it."

"I'm looking for a table."

"I collect brown-and-white crockery and beer cans."

"My grandmother had one just like it."

Extra credit question:

"May I use your restroom?"

If you can read and interpret one of the following ads you are already one of the most knowledgeable authorities on your block. If you can read and interpret more than two, you are a *budding* national authority.

For Sale:

Pine, step-back cupboard, sixteen lights, original paint, signed hinges, c. 1840, provenance available.

Ovoid 3 gal. jug, incised decoration, impressed mark, slight hairline at base.

Scrubbed top table, walnut, secondary wood is pine, pin construction, early red paint, c. 1850.

If any of the words or terms in these rather typical ads gave you pause, a little homework is in order before you venture forth with checkbook in hand.

Since we live in an age of instant coffee, weight loss, credit, and pudding, and there is a national mania to have personal problems resolved by adopting instant programs of pop psychology, it is also possible to gather knowledge quickly and painlessly for fun and profit. We have designed this brief section to allow the reader to become an instant national authority on country antiques.

Albany slip: A mixture of chocolate brown clay and water used to coat the interiors of crocks, jugs, and other pieces of stoneware.

Architectural cupboard: A cupboard or case piece of furniture that was originally built into a house. As "early" homes are demolished, architectural pieces may find their way into antiques shops.

Bee: The New Town, Connecticut, *Bee* publishes an "Antiques and Arts Weekly" that includes interesting articles about all phases of the antiques' world from auctions to show openings and personality sketches of dealers, collectors, and authors.

Blind front — glazed front: A "blind front" cupboard contains no "lights" or glass. A cupboard with solid wooden doors or a "blind front" is usually less valuable than a similar "glazed front" cupboard with individual panes of glass or "lights."

Blanket chest — blanket box: A blanket chest differs from a blanket box because it contains one or more drawers. The drawers normally add significantly to the value of the blanket chest over the blanket box that has no drawers.

Breadboard ends: A breadboard end is a strip of wood that is nailed or mortised to each end of a table top to keep the top from warping.

Circa: A term used in connection with providing an approximate date for a given artifact. Often the term may mean plus or minus ten or fifteen years from the date given.

Decorated stoneware: During the nineteenth century stoneware was decorated with five major techniques. Each method of decoration can provide some insights into the approximate age of the piece of stoneware.

Incised: Decoration scratched into the surface of the clay with a piece of wire or a sharp tool. C. 1800-1830.

Brush painted: Using a fine brush to paint cobalt slip onto the surface of the stoneware. C. 1830-1890.

Slip cup: Spreading cobalt slip with a tool similar to one a cake decorator would use. The process leaves a slip trail on the surface of the stoneware that can easily be felt if a hand is rubbed across the decoration. C. 1840-1860.

Impressed: The name of the pottery was often stamped or impressed into the neck of the jug to indicate where it was made. After the late 1870s some potteries stamped

small animal or bird impressions into the clay for a trademark.

Stenciling: A great deal of stoneware was stenciled rather than brush painted after 1875. The costs and time involved in decorating each piece reached a point where alternative techniques were needed. The stencil was placed on the crock or jug and paint quickly brushed over it. This technique was used well into the twentieth century.

Early-late: These two terms are extremely relative and can create a great deal of confusion and frustration. There are "early" pieces of stoneware (Commeraw, Crolius) and "late" (Peoria, Red Wing). There are "early" Windsor chairs from the late eighteenth century and "late" Windsor chairs from the early twentieth century that were made for fire stations and libraries.

Early paint — original paint — late paint: The first coat of paint on a cupboard is the original paint. Rarely does a painted piece of furniture survive in its original form without being repainted at some point. A cupboard in "early paint" still contains *at least* one coat of paint underneath. Most country furniture was repainted periodically as wear became excessive. "Late paint" is a relative term that could mean the last coat was applied in 1879 or 1979. "Late paint" may be a cause for concern when a collector sees it in relation to a piece he is choosing.

Garth's: An auction house located in Delaware, Ohio, that is considered by most collectors to be the premier auction house for collections and estates featuring country and New England antiques in Middle America. Catalogs of each sale are available on a subscription basis. Telephone and mail bids may be made.

Practice sentence: "One sold for (less, more, about the same) in the (Garfield Goose, Mr. Bill, Doc Savage) auction last month at Garth's."

Gould: Mary Earle Gould's *Early American Woodenware* was originally published in 1942. It is the definitive book on American woodenware and kitchen antiques.

Practice sentence: "I saw a similar one in Gould's book but it was (larger, smaller, in better condition)."

Maine Antiques Digest: The most popular of the monthly newspapers dealing primarily with New England and country antiques. M.A.D. is published eleven times a year from Waldoboro, Maine.

Married: A piece of furniture is said to be "married" when two or more individual and distinct pieces are joined to form a single cupboard, highboy, or desk.

Practice sentence: "The top and bottom of that cupboard wouldn't be a marriage, would it?"

Molded rather than thrown: The competition between potteries reached the point in the late nineteenth century that only large potteries could possibly survive. The common use of glass containers and mechanical refrigeration destroyed most of the remaining markets for stoneware. The potteries were to turn to mecha-

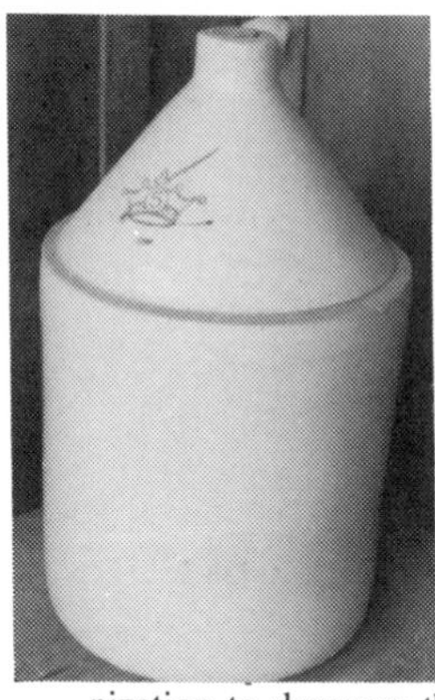

nization to decrease their costs. In the 1870s pottery that was produced in molds rather than individually hand thrown on a wheel became a major problem for small local potteries. After 1885 most of the stoneware was molded rather than thrown.

Ohio Antiques Review: A paper similar in form to the M.A.D. but concentrated more on the antiques happenings in Pennsylvania, Ohio, and the Middle West. The O.A.R. is published monthly from Worthington, Ohio.

Ovoid: The ovoid form usually dates a jug as being produced prior to 1840. Most contain a minimum of cobalt decoration. As the nineteenth century wore on, potteries gradually made the sides of their wares more cylindrical in shape.

Patina: Patina refers to the quality of the surface of a piece of furniture or woodenware. The development of a patina is a natural process produced through use, abuse, age, wear, dirt, sunlight, and luck. The patina of a table top may be compared to a young child's innocence. Once it is disturbed or altered, it is gone forever.

Pieced out: A close look at the legs of a sampling of tables and chairs will provide some insight into the ''piecing out'' process. Many work or farm tables were constructed to meet the needs of generations of families four to six inches shorter than most contemporary families. To market these tables or chairs it is crucial to add several inches to each leg.

Played with: A country antique that has been ''played with'' could have been ''married,'' ''pieced out,'' had drawers removed or added, or been repainted. Often, people buy a particular antique emotionally and not intellectually. They are overwhelmed by the apparent rarity or alleged age and do not search the piece diligently for its warts and repaired limbs. Six months later when the emotions have cooled, the buyer sees the wire nails, the lack of wear where wear should be, and the new paint.

Provenance: Provenance refers to the history of successive ownership that goes with a particular antique. Rarely does a collector receive an accurate provenance with his purchase. The dealer who sells the piece is only one in a long line of owners who have passed the piece down the line.

Secondary wood: The term secondary wood refers to the wood that a casual observer does not see when he looks at a cherry or walnut cupboard. The pine or poplar used for drawer sides and bottoms and the back of the cupboard is referred to as the secondary wood. Early joiners did mot use wood that was in limited supply for these areas. The soft pine or poplar was much more plentiful and easier to work with so it was a standard procedure to use either as a secondary wood.

Scrubbed top: On most early tables the top was originally painted the same color as the rest of the piece. After each meal the top was carefully scrubbed down to remove the remnants of the meal. With each scrubbing the harsh home-

made soaps removed a little paint. Eventually all the paint was wasted away and a bleached table top remained.

J. NORTON & CO. BENNINGTON VT. 1859-1861

J.&E. NORTON
BENNINGTON VT.

1850-1861

Signed: If an eighteenth century side chair carries its maker's name burned or branded into the underside of the seat, its value is increased. A piece of "signed" stoneware may have the pottery where it was produced impressed into the clay just below the neck of a jug. It is possible to date a piece of stoneware by the impressed signature or mark. We have in-

WHITE'S UTICA
C. 1880s

cluded six "signed" pieces and their approximate date of production. Potteries opened, closed, and changed owners so often that precise dating is almost impossible.

POLAND MINERAL
SPRING WATER
35 CONGRESS ST.
BOSTON

This is the mark of the business for whom the piece was produced. It would take a Boston city directory to date the business and the pottery.

LYONS
(New York)

1870s

C.W. BRAUN
BUFFALO, N.Y.

1860s

Step-back: A cupboard with a "step-back" is set back or recessed 4″ to 10″ from the bottom section. This provides a shelf or open storage or work area between the top and bottom halves of the cupboard.

3 Furniture

The difficulty in determining the value of country antiques is complicated by the lack of an even distribution across the nation. Our point is made by comparing a randomly selected (almost) auction from a small town newspaper in Illinois with similar ads from the New Town (Conn.) *Bee* published the same week. The Illinois ad lists the following:

Press-back chairs
Nice salt and pepper collection
Beam bottles
Display case
Pocket knives
Cherry (?) dresser
Brass (?) bucket
Dated fruit jars
Several stone jars
Horsehide rug
Gone with the Wind lamp base
Sad iron set

The Connecticut newspaper lists the following from an Auburn, Massachusetts, auction held September 20, 1979:

Set of five thumb-back stenciled chairs with original paint
Pine drop-front desk, nicely scalloped
Early pine box with dome top and heart handles
Pilgrim century one-drawer tavern table
Shaker-style tea table

A September 21, 1979 auction in Bolton, Massachusetts, included:

Queen Ann inlaid lowboy
Painted sea chest with ship portrait
Two bow-back Windsor armchairs
American Pilgrim chest of drawers
Jacquard coverlet
Running horse weathervane

The two Massachusetts auctions are typical of almost forty that were advertised in the same issue of the *Bee*'s "Antique and Arts Weekly." Any one of those auctions would have been considered a major event among serious collectors in many parts of Illinois, Iowa, Arizona, or California. Note especially the terms that were used in the ads with little or no need for explanations:

thumb back
scalloped
stenciled
original paint
dome top
heart handles
Shaker-style
tavern table
bow-back Windsor

Many weekend collectors in much of the Midwest, Plains, and Far West are not familiar with these terms because they have not encountered the type of items with which they would be found. They are much more aware of oak iceboxes, Hoosier kitchen cabinets, fruit jars, and depression glass. Even these items have become scarce and draw auction crowds when they appear on sale bills in many areas.

The obvious explanation is the migration patterns in which the nation was settled. The east-to-west settlement took almost three hundred years. The pine cupboards that were carried by Conestoga wagons from Pennsylvania to Illinois or Iowa in the two decades between 1840 and 1860 were eventually replaced in the late 1870s and early 1880s by factory-made late Victorian or early oak produced by major manufacturers and sold through mail order emporiums in Chicago, St. Louis, Baltimore, and New York. During the last quarter of the nineteenth century almost every community had a store that marketed factory-produced household goods and conveniences ranging from bedroom suites to cast iron soap holders.

The handcrafted products of rural New England became an embarassment to people entering the twentieth century. Chairs, beds, and tables of maple and pine were shunted to the refuse pile or the barn and had to wait another fifty years to be rediscovered and recherished.

The farther west the prairie pilgrims traveled from New Hampshire or New York the less they were able to carry with them. Few household furnishings from the East Coast made it to California with the original owners.

Psychologists are quick to point out that in times of economic difficulty or national crisis there is a tendency to look back to the allegedly happier times of a more peaceful period. As will be pointed out several times, the national print media has recently embraced the "country look" in home furnishings. The majority of the magazines that are devoted to shaping taste in interior design feature monthly articles on utilizing early textiles, kitchen artifacts, baskets and pine furniture in a variety of urban and rural settings.

The increased awareness of country antiques by a wide variety of emerging "collectors" has pushed prices of previously affordable antiques through the roof. We recently attended an antiques show in search of a painted dry sink. We found one similar to many we used to see several years ago for $200-$275. This example was now offered for $875.

As more people become aware of country furniture and as collectors and others become aware as investors, prices will continue to multiply.

In the late 1960s friends who had been collecting since the 1940s commented to us many times how amazed they were at the expense of early things they previously could have purchased for a few dollars.

We now look back on the 1960s and are shocked at the things we failed to buy because of their cost at the time.

We are repeatedly asked where to find the best buys in country furniture. The answer to the question brings to mind an opportunity to buy a cupboard in a basement and a dry sink out of the loft of a dairy barn.

The obvious trick to building a collection is to occasionally buy the right thing in the wrong place at the right price. It is purchases like that which keep the collecting fires burning on less successful trips.

Identifying Country Chairs

Half spindle, thumb-back, or rabbit-ear

Spindle-back

Arrow-back

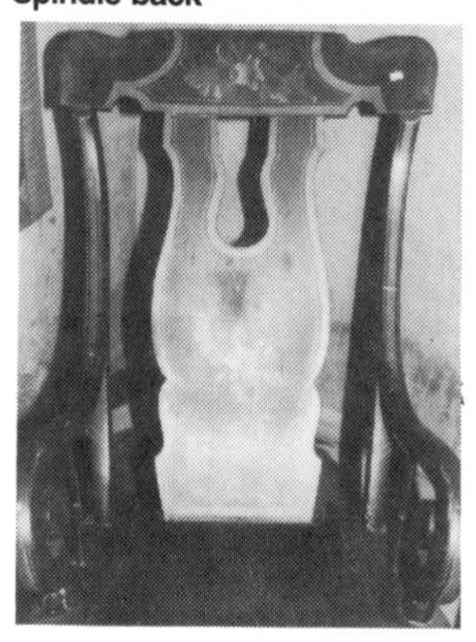

Bootjack splat with decorated crest rail

Ladder-back or slat-back

Salem rocker with spindle-back, decorated crest rail, c. 1830-1835

Stencilled crest rail

Shaker tilter

Bucket bench, wood box
Pine, early red paint, found in Ohio, c. 1880.
Value: $550-$650.

This example is unusual because it has a wood box. Bucket benches were used for storing washday supplies and were generally kept on the back porch. The round nails date it from the late nineteenth century. Pieces of this type should be examined carefully, because the heavy use they were put to often makes them appear earlier than they actually are.

Bucket bench
Pine, early red paint, 24″ high 44″ long, found in Ohio, c. 1860-1870.
Value: $370-$400.

Another uncommon form for a bucket bench. It appears to be a dry sink, because of its design and zinc-lined trough. The two shelves below held soap, rags, and brushes. Pine was typically used in constructing water or bucket benches. This example retains much of its early milk base paint.

Bucket bench
Pine, early red paint, uncommon form, found in Pennsylvania, c. 1840.
Value: $450-$550.

This bucket bench originally had a bar across the front of the top shelf. Like many pieces of early furniture, it had several generations of paint on it when purchased. The coat that preceded the red was oak graining applied with one of the tin combs that were used in the late 1800s.

Bucket bench
Pine, 30″ high, unpainted, Ohio, c. 1880-1900.
Value: $100-$125.

This small bench has bootjack ends and cross stretcher supports. It is held together by screws, rather than the round headed nails one would suspect.

Bucket bench
Pine, in old gray paint, possibly Shaker, c. 1850-1860.
Value: $950-$1,150.

This piece is an uncommon form for a bucket bench. It contains a single drawer and a storage compartment with double doors.

Bucket bench
Pine, mortised construction, early green paint, Pennsylvania, c. 1830-1840.
Value: $210-$225.

This bench measures 36″ long x 29″ high and was used on a table or dry sink.

Dry sink
Pine, unusual extended trough for a pump, Ohio, c. 1860
Value: $900-$1,000.

Six-drawer Shaker spice chest
Old red stain, turned knobs, c. 1870-1880.
Value: $300-$350.

This early dry sink in red paint was found in Ohio and dates from the mid-1800s. Collectors find more dry sinks in Ohio, Indiana, and Illinois than any other section of the country. They date from 1850 until well into the twentieth century. Most sinks are of poplar or pine, with late examples of oak turning up occasionally at flea markets or closing-out farm sales.

Dry sink
Pine, single drawer, c. 1870.
Value: $475-$525.

The pine sink was purchased in eastern Indiana. It has a single drawer for soap or kitchen utensils. The drawer pull is a late replacement, and the work area above has been repaired.

Dry sink
Pine, in old green paint, c. 1870-1880, found in Ohio.
Value: $500-$550.

This is a conventional Midwestern sink in design. It was probably painted for the last time fifty to seventy-five years ago. The zinc lining has been removed and Rockingham pulls added at some point. This example was found in Ohio and dates from the late 1800s.

Dry sink
Pine, green and red-paint, Illinois, c. 1870.
Value: $650-$750.

Another Midwestern form of the dry sink that dates from the mid-1800s.

Dry sink
Pine, refinished, found in Connecticut, c. 1870-1880.
Value: $325-$350.
(Larry Troyer Collection.)

Apothecary chest
Pine, original paint and hardware, found in Massachusetts, c. 1850.
Value: $1,750-$2,000.

Apothecary chest
Pine, purchased in Ohio, originally from New England, early paint, c. 1840-1850.
Value: $1,750-$2,000.

Bedside table
Pine, refinished, New England, c. 1870.
Value: $300-$350.

Tables of this type were used in bedrooms for holding pitcher and bowl sets. This example was originally covered with green paint, but was refinished about twenty years ago. The value would increase by $200-$250 if the table had its original paint.

Linen press or storage cupboard
Pine, early red paint, Pennsylvania, c. 1840-1850.
Value: $850-$1,000.

A linen press is a storage piece for blankets and household linens. Cracks similar to the one in the door generally have little significance to the value of early country furniture.

Miniature chests
Pine, early green and blue paint, Pennsylvania, c. 1860-1870.
Value: $200-$225 each.

Miniature chest
Pine, early green paint, Pennsylvania, c. 1860-1870.
Value: $200-$225.

This is a close-up of the chest at the top of the stack at left. It measures 5″ high x 5½″ deep x 9½″ long.

Immigrant's chest or blanket chest
Pine, early red paint, Pennsylvania, c. 1840, dimensions: 48″ long x 28″ high x 24″ deep.
Value: $600-$700.

Many times a piece of furniture of uncommon size has its value limited by the difficulty it creates in trying to use it in a conventional home.

Immigrant's trunk
Pine, painted green, signed "Friedrich Ruffel," c. mid-nineteenth century.
Value: $125-$150.

Sea captain's chest
Pine, wrought iron hardware, red paint, c. 1820.
Value: $375-$400.

Close-up of dovetails on sea captain's chest.

Chopping table
Pine, original finish, Illinois, c. 1880-1900, dimensions: 35½″ wide x 28″ high x 65½″ long.
Value: $500-$550.

Comb-decorated blanket chest
Pine, early red and mustard paint, Ohio, c. 1860.
Value: $550-$650.
(Hilliard Collection, Provo, Utah)

Decorated blanket chest
Pine, mustard and orange paint, Ohio, c. 1860, dimensions: 48″ long x 19″ x 28″ high.
Value: $500-$600.

Blanket chest
Pine, refinished, New York State, c. 1870-1875.
Value: $250-$300.

Immigrant's suitcase
Pine and maple, painted blue, c. 1840s.
Value: $200-$240.

Blanket chest
Pine, early blue paint, dovetailed, Pennsylvania, c. 1850.
Value: $500-$550.

Storage box
Initialed "E.F.D." and dated 1876, pine, painted green.
Value: $125-$140.

Jelly or preserve cupboard
Pine, refinished, Ohio.
Value: $200-$250.

This small (35″ high) and crudely constructed storage cupboard was found in northeastern Ohio. It contains two shelves and carries traces of its original red paint.

Kitchen cupboard
Pine, refinished, storage piece or "jelly" cupboard.
Value: $550-$650.

Step-back cupboard
Pine, early red paint, two-piece construction, Ohio, c. 1840.
Value: $1,300-$1,500.

Open cupboard
Pine, refinished, c. 1830-1850.
Value: $1,000-$1,200.

Step-back cupboard
Pine and wild cherry, sixteen lights, Ohio, c. 1840-1850.
Value: $1,400-$1,600.
(Dameron Collection)

This two-piece cupboard originally was covered with two coats of deep brown paint. The lights or panes of glass appear to be original.

Blind front cupboard
Pine with traces of original red paint, replaced "shoe" feet, c. 1860.
Value: $875-$1,100.

Jam or jelly cupboard
Pine, early blue paint, New York State, c. 1840-1850.
Value: $1,500-$2,000.

The most desirable color of early furniture for most collectors is blue. Blue paint on a bucket or piece of furniture usually adds 40 to 50 percent to the value.

This cupboard is an unusual form with a display or work surface on top and two large storage areas below.

Kitchen cupboard
Pine, refinished, "jelly" cupboard form.
Value: $475-$550.

Country secretary
Walnut, pull-out writing slide, two pieces, six lights, made in Watseka, Illinois, c. 1850.
Value: $850-$1,000.

Schoolmaster's desk
Pine, early red paint, Pennsylvania, c. 1830-1840.
Value: $800-$900.

Bedside table
Pine, early paint, Ohio, c. 1870-1880.
Value: $275-$325.

The value of this piece is increased by the turned legs, early paint and additional work on the drawer front. The knob is a late replacement.

Small bench
Pine, worn green paint, Pennsylvania, c. 1860-1880.
Value: $325-$375.

Wagon seat
Pine and maple, refinished, splint seat, New England, c. 1830-1840.
Value: $425-$450. In early paint, $700-$800.

Chairs of this type were used in horsedrawn passenger and farm wagons in the early 1800s. They provided a place to sit on the way to town or church and could be removed and carried inside after arrival.

Deacon's bench or settle
Maple and pine, refinished, length 72″, c. 1870.
Value: $400-$450.

Similar benches in a variety of lengths ranging from 4′ to 14′ were manufactured and sold to churches, town halls, and shopkeepers for use in front of their emporiums from the 1850s through 1900.

Recitation bench
Pine, original unpainted finish, from an Amish school in Ohio, c. 1850.
Value: $550-$650.

This bench is 5½′ long and the plank seat is 13″ off the ground. It was used as a bench for primary age children to recite their lessons in front of a class filled with their bored peers.

Chopping block
Maple, refinished, turned, round legs, c. 1880-1900.
Value: $400-$450.
(Spilman-Cutler collection, Knoxville, Ill.)

Work table
Early blue-gray paint, maple and pine, scrubbed top, found in Ohio, c. 1850.
Value: $400-$450.

This country work table has a two-board top, pegged sides, and turned legs. Use of pine and maple in a piece of furniture is not unusual. Often, several woods were used because the table or chair was painted soon after its construction.

Chest of drawers
Oak graining over pine, New England, c. 1860.
Value: $700-$750.

When oak regained its popularity in the late 1800s, there was a rush to simulate oak grain on many pieces that had been purchased a generation or two earlier. Many examples from the early 1800s were given a stylish paint job in the 1880s.

Chopping block
Walnut on maple legs, 9″ thick, Indiana, c. 1860(?).
Value: $100-$110.

A small block is almost impossible to date accurately, because construction techniques changed little for a period of more than 250 years. It could be as early as the 1700s, or as late as the early 1900s.

Blocks of this type were used for separating chickens from their heads.

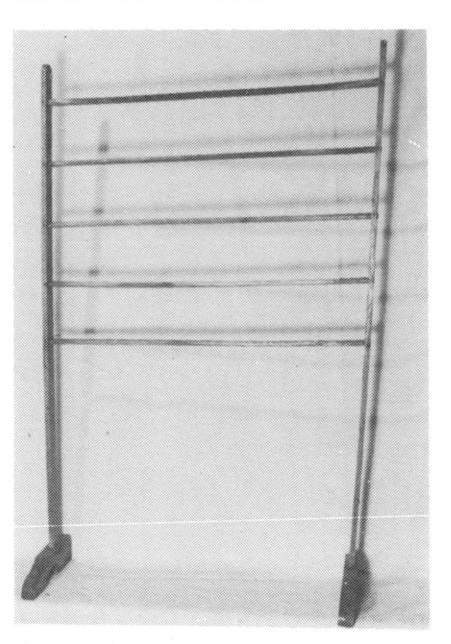

Towel rack
Maple, shoe feet, found in Ohio, c. 1900.
Value: $85-$100.

Quilt or coverlet rack
Maple, factory-made, c. 1880-1900.
Value: $90-$100.
(Skinner collection)

Country store coffee bin
Pine, red paint, stenciled label, replaced bottom board, c. 1900.
Value: $150-$200.

Staved storage barrel
Pine, early blue paint, iron bands, 28″ high, c. 1870.
Value: $475-$500.

Small immigrant's trunk
Pine, worn top, early green bottom, Scandinavian, c. 1840-1850.
Value: $200-$225.

This trunk measures 30″ long x 8″ high x 14″ deep. It was brought to the United States in the mid-1800s by a Swedish immigrant and was found in Wisconsin.

Slat-back kitchen chair
Maple and pine, splint seat, blue-gray paint, c. 1840.
Value: $150-$175.
Set of four in similar condition, $800-$850.

Bannister-back side chair
Tiger maple, sausage-turned legs, replaced rush seat, New York State, c. 1830.
Value: $375-$425.

Slat-back side chair
Pine, chestnut, and maple, replaced splint seat, Ohio, c. 1860.
Value: $85-$100.

Slat-back side chair
Maple, splint seat, refinished, New York State, c. 1850.
Value: $75-$85.
Set of four in similar condition, $400-$425.

Stenciled side chairs
Mixture of woods, pine plank seat, Pennsylvania, c. 1850-1860.
Value: $70-$75.
Set of four in *mint* original paint, $650-$750.

These chairs were originally sold in sets of six to twelve. Sets of chairs in good condition with the early decoration intact are hard to find. These examples have reached the point where they will have to be stripped or repainted. If repainting is the process chosen, before and after pictures should be taken to document their age and the original decoration.

Arrow-back settee
Black paint, pine and maple, New York State, c. 1830.
Value: $700-$750.

Boston fiddle-back rocking chair
Early red and black decoration, stenciling, freehand flowers, found in Illinois, c. 1860-1875.
Value: $400-$450.

Hoop-back Windsor armchair
Maple and pine, simply turned legs, probably English.
Value: $200-$225.

Slat-back child's armchair
Splint seat, early stenciling and black paint, c. 1860.
Value: $150-$175.

Loop-back Windsor side chair
American, maple with pine plank seat, refinished, c. 1830.
Value: $125-$150.
Set of four refinished chairs, $500-$525.
Set of four chairs in old paint, $800-$850.

Slat-back armchair
Replaced splint seat, refinished, New York State, early turnings, c. 1802-1830.
Value: $175-$200.

Slat-back kitchen chair
Pine and maple, refinished, "rabbit ears," c. 1880.
Value: $85-$100.
Set of four refinished, $500-$525.

Corner cupboard
Pine, refinished, dimensions: 73" high x 33" wide, Maine.
Value: $950-$1,100. In original paint, $1,500-$2,000. (Fedder collection.)

Rod-back kitchen chair
Maple, pine plank seat, Midwestern c. 1850-1860.
Value: $75-$90.

Simply constructed side chairs are often described and sold as Shaker. Merely because a chair has no "superfluous" decoration does not make it Shaker. Collectors should consult Meader's *Illustrated Guide to Shaker Furniture* for an authoritative background on the Shaker arts.

Rod-back Windsor highchair
Maple with pine plank seat, late paint, New England, c. 1840.
Value: $200-$225. In early paint, $350-$425.

Child's Windsor hoop-back armchair from England
Maple 2″ pine plank seat, H stretcher, c. 1800-1820.
Value: $350-$375.

The legs of the English Windsors have a much tighter angle to floor than American chairs.

It is interesting to note the difference between a hoop-back and loop-back chair. Hoop-back Windsors have a bar across the center of the spindles.

American Windsor chairs are considerably rarer and more costly than their English counterparts.

Printer's stool
Maple, 42″ high, factory produced, never painted, c. 1890-1900.
Value: $65-$80.

Milking stool
Difficult to date, 18″ high, found in Pennsylvania.
Value: $55-$70.

Low-post cannonball bed
Maple and pine, New York State, c, 1870-1875.
Value: $550-$650.

Low-post beds have carved headboards and footboards with turned posts. All four posts are about the same height. Most low-post beds are constructed of combinations of pine, cherry, chestnut, maple, and birch.

Low-post bed
Maple, painted red, rope-type, found in New York State, c. 1830.
Value: $575-$625.

Low-post cannonball bed
Maple, walnut, pine, remnants of red paint, rope-type construction to hold mattress, Ohio, c. 1840-1860.
Value: $550-$650.

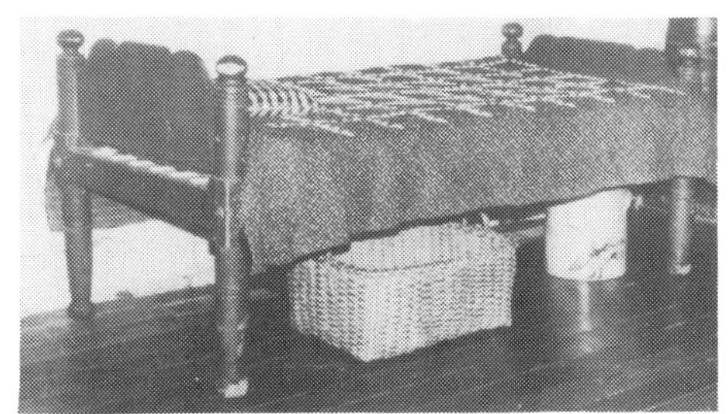

Low-post bed
Pine and maple, painted redrope-type, found in Maine,

c. 1830-1840
Value: $700-$775.

Low-post bed
Maple, original finish, rope-type, c. 1860-1870.
Value: $700-$775.

High-post bed
Walnut, original finish, rope-type, c. 1860-1870.
Value: $900-$1,000.

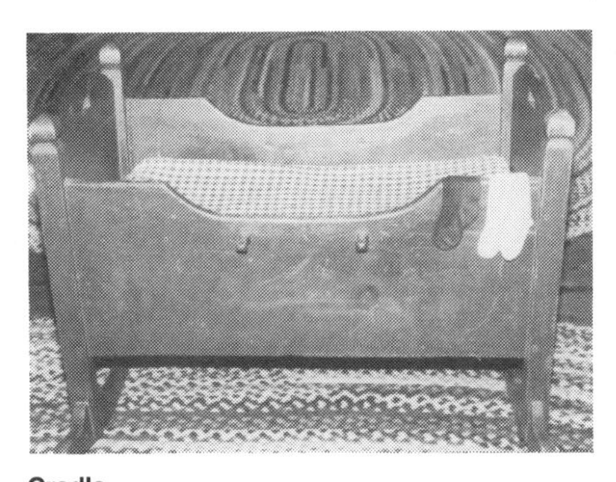

Cradle
Pine, painted red, c. 1830.
Value: $600-$675.

The pegs protuding from the side were used to tie a rope across the top of the cradle to keep its contents from rolling onto the floor during an especially bad dream.

Cradle
Pine, open end, mustard exterior paint, uncommon finials and carved side decoration, New England, c. 1830-1840.
Value: $475-$550.

Dough box
Pine, Ohio, refinished, joined with square nails, c. 1850-1860.
Value: $300-$325. Original paint: $500-$575.

Document box
Pine, sponge-decorated yellow and brown paint, New Hampshire, c. 1830-1840.
Value: $300-$350.

Small food storage chest
Dimensions: 15″ long x 12″ deep x 13″ high, old blue exterior, worn red interior, staved construction early iron bands, found in Wisconsin, probably Scandinavian, c. 1800.
Value: $350-$400.

Candlestand
Tripod form, maple, New England, cleated two-board top, c. 1800.
Value: $500-$575.

Tilt-top or tip-top table
Cherry, turned shaft, tripod legs, New England, c. 1800-1820.
Value: $600-$650.

Work table
Pine, scrubbed top, unusual carved gallery, single drawer, found in Pennsylvania, red base, c. 1840-1860.
Value: $300-$325.

Sawbuck table
Dimensions: 28½" high x 20" deep x 32½" long, pegged-top construction, pine, original finish, maple supports, c. 1820.
Value: $500-$575.

Horseshoer's box
Pine, wrought iron handle, early red paint, two boxes for nails, c. 1870-1890.
Value: $135-$150.

Cricket table
Pine, refinished, c. mid-nineteenth century.
Value: $250-$275.

Rocking chair
Spindle-back, maple and pine, refinished, uncommon form, replaced rush seat, c. 1840.
Value: $220-$240.

Clock
Signed, "Lumas Watson, Cincinnati, Ohio," pine, refinished case, original face and works, 1810-1840.
Value: $2,800-$3,200.

Spinning wheel
Pine and maple, original finish, c. mid-nineteenth century.
Value: $240-$260.

Storage cupboard
Pine, refinished, found in New York State, c. 1840.
Value: $350-$400.

Early Victorian chest of drawers
Tiger maple, made in an early factory, c. 1840.
Value: $550-$575.

4 *Kitchen and Hearth Antiques*

Rural America was basically a handcrafted society until the mid-1800s when industrialization and mass production began to affect the tastes of the American family.

The first 250 years of colonization, revolution, and immigration before 1850 found the kitchen and hearth tools used in cooking produced by a local blacksmith, a tinsmith, or a husband handy with a carving knife and a supply of pine and maple.

Stores came to even the remotest village after the mid-point of the nineteenth century with large supplies of factory-made hardware, stoves, buckets, tableware, and packaged groceries.

It is increasingly difficult for collectors today to find early woodenware and iron cooking utensils. In the late 1960s, the problem was compounded by a large influx of wooden spoons, stools, baskets, food molds, buckets, and a wide variety of early iron from Spain, Portugal, Eastern Europe, and Mexico.

These imports were brought into the United States in such large quantities and offered at such reasonable prices that a number of obvious problems were created for collectors of American kitchen antiques. It might be wise for collectors to obtain a copy of the importers' catalogs and learn the hearth and kitchen items available.

Kitchen pieces in metal, wood, or pottery have more of a standard nationwide value than early furniture. They are easier to use in the Kansas split-level than a high-back dry sink in early worn paint, and certainly easier to transport from Vermont or New Hampshire. Many collectors become interested at a point in their lives when they have already furnished their homes and have room only for decorative accessories.

Nest of pantry boxes
Early original paint, round boxes, excellent condition, c. 1880.
Value: $50-$95 each, depending on size.

In the past few years pantry boxes have been "discovered" and prices have soared. Painted boxes are at least two to three times more expensive than refinished or unpainted boxes. The nests or stocks that collectors build are "put together." An original nest in old paint is almost impossible to obtain.

Pine utility box
Painted red, maple handle, c. 1880-1900.
Value: $70-$80.

Scouring box
Box, scouring board tin pumice holder, c. 1860-1870.
Value: $60-$70

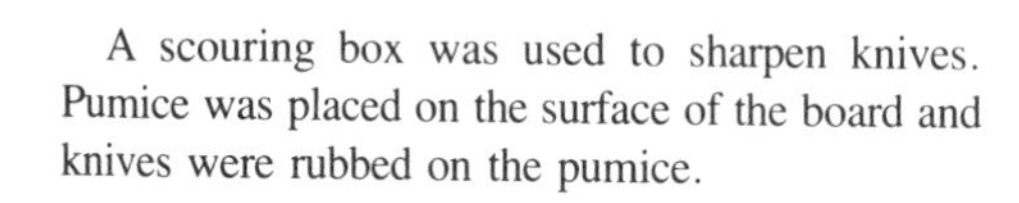

A scouring box was used to sharpen knives. Pumice was placed on the surface of the board and knives were rubbed on the pumice.

Dough tray
Pine, painted red, found in Vermont, c. 1850.
Value: $125-$140.

Carrier
Pine, New England, c. late eighteeneth century, original unpainted finish.
Value: $200-$225.

Maple bowl
Hand-hewn maple, c. 1840.
Value: $85-$95.

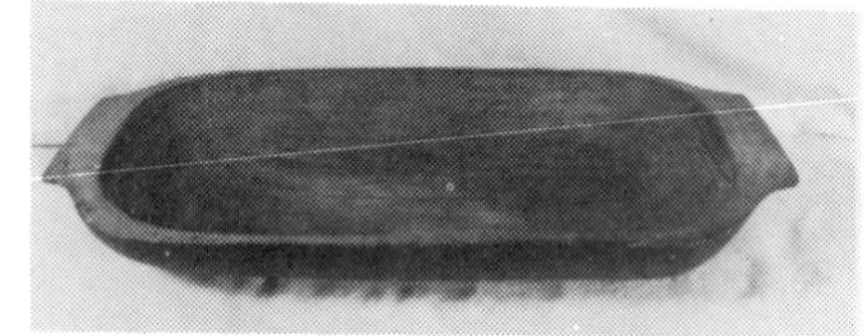

Chopping bowl
Maple, early blue paint in worn condition, c. 1860-65.
Value: $100-$110.

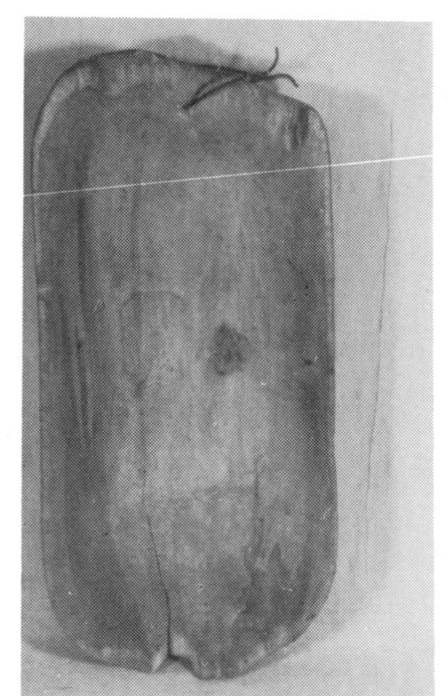

Chopping bowl
Found in Kentucky, pine, "as found" condition, c. 1850.
Value: $50-$65.

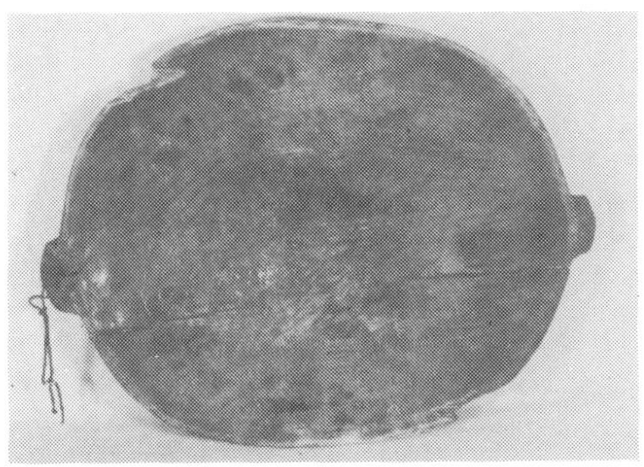

Chopping bowl
Maple, early form, "ear" handles, c. 1830.
Value: $90-$95.

Work bowl
Maple, 38″ long x 20″ wide, hand-hewn, c. 1850.
Value: $125-$145.

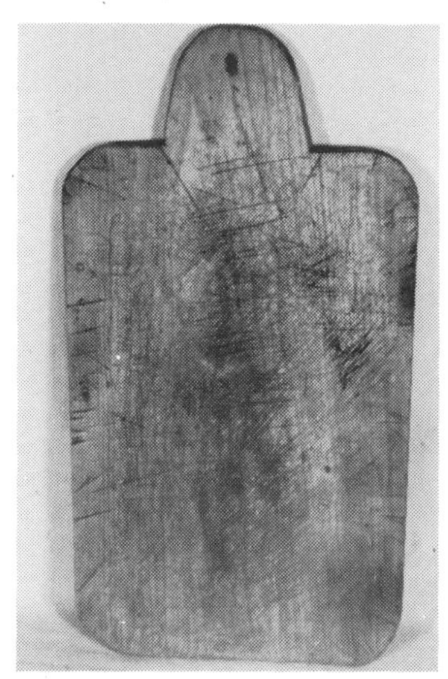

Chopping board
Pine, "as found" condition, difficult to date.
Value: $40-$45.

Pieces that have had heavy use are difficult to date accurately. Chopping boards in this form were in use throughout the nineteenth and well into the twentieth century.

Burl bowl
Found in New England, 14″ diameter, c. 1830-1850.
Value: $500-$525.

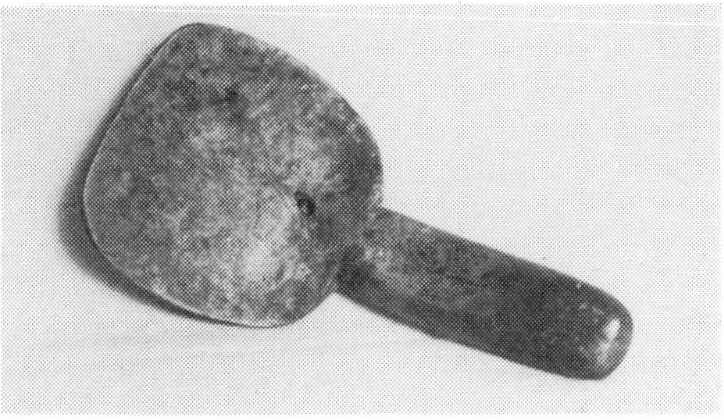

Burl butter worker, hand-formed
Found in New England, c. 1830.
Value: $175-$200.

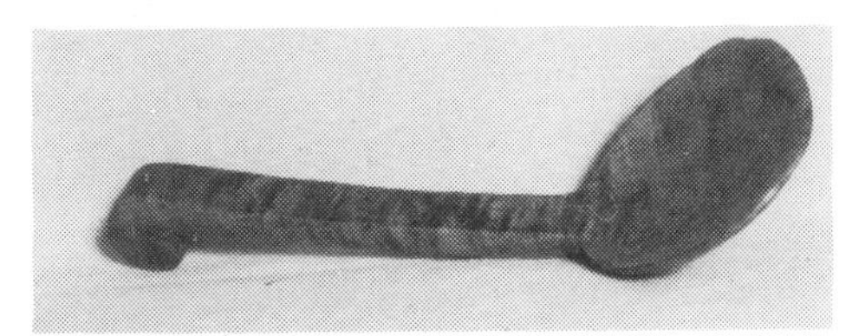

Butter worker
Tiger maple, hand-formed, c. 1840.
Value: $90-$100.

Butter workers were used to "work" or press excess water out of freshly churned butter.

Butter worker
Maple, factory-made, c. 1870.
Value: $20-$25.

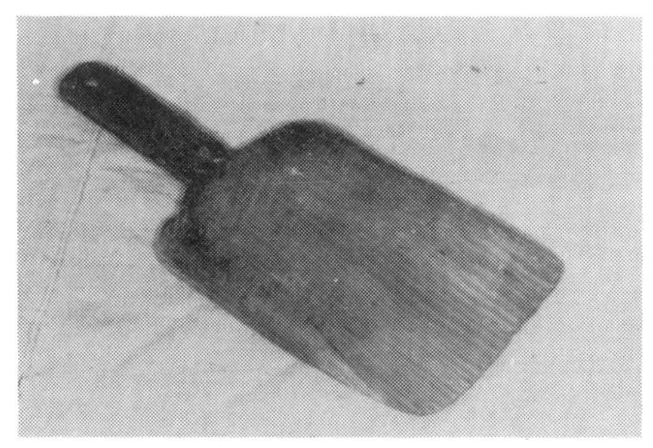

Peel
Pine, found in Ohio, used to remove baked goods from oven, c. 1860-1870.
Value: $45-$55.

Pantry boxes
Early paint, nailed joints, 6″ diameter and 7″ diameter, c. 1880.
Value: $45-$55.

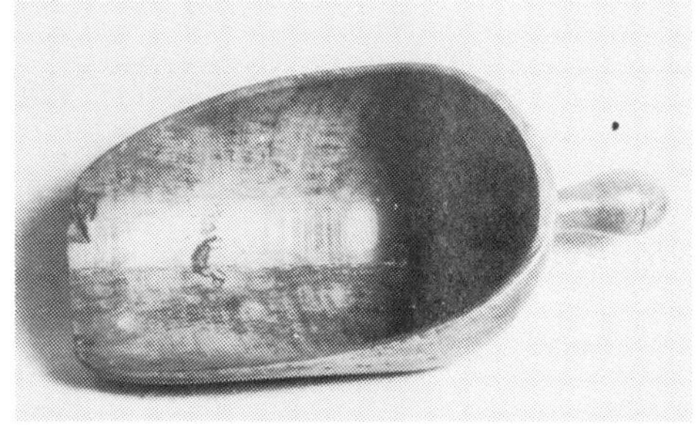

Scoop
Maple, formed from single piece of wood, used with flour or sugar, c, 1870.
Value: $100-$125.

Cheese draining board
Maple, breadboard ends, homemade, c. 1860.
Value: $125-$150.

Breadboard ends are two strips of wood nailed to the top and bottom of the cheese drainer to keep it from warping. They are also commonly found on tables and chopping boards.

Miniature cookie cutter
Tin heart, maple handle, found in southern New York State, 1½″ high x 2″ deep, c. 1830-1840.
Value: $150-$175.

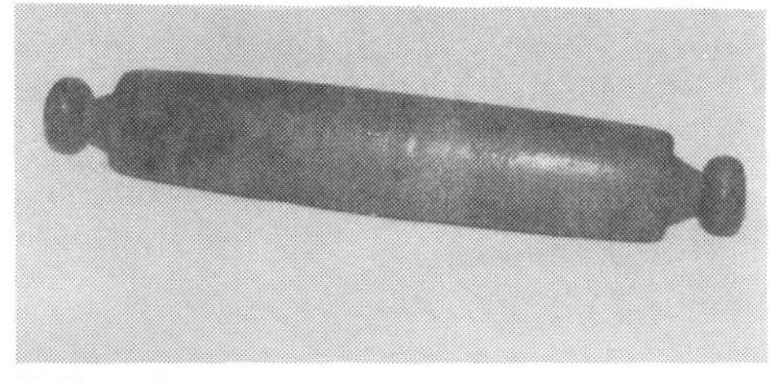

Rolling pin
Early form, maple, c. 1860.
Value: $50-$55.

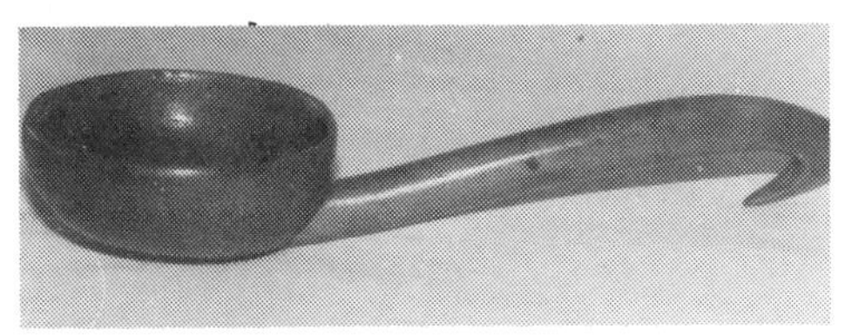

Wooden ladle
Maple, hand-carved, refinished, c. mid-nineteenth century.
Value: $95-$110.

Rolling pin, butter worker, butter molds
Maple, late nineteenth century.
Values: Butter worker - $20-$25.
Miniature butter mold - $40-$45.
Rolling pin - $30-$35.
Box butter mold - $55-$60.

Handcrafted American woodenware from the nineteenth century is almost impossible to find. The early kitchen utensils were used until they were cracked or broken and replaced. Relatively few examples have survived. There is a wealth of European woodenware that is constantly being imported and offered to collectors.

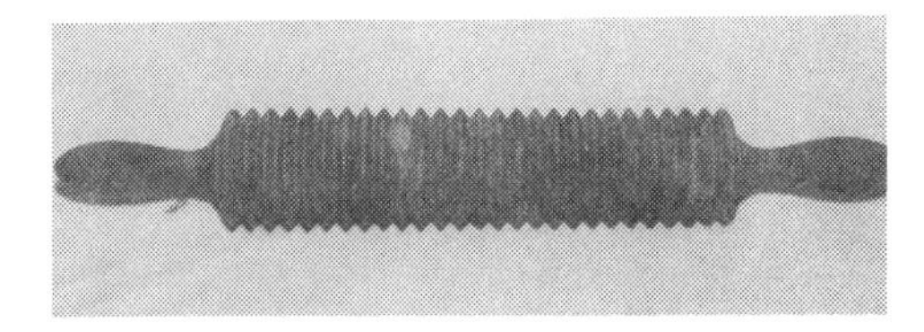

Rolling pin
Factory made, maple, c. 1880-1910.
Value: $30-$35.

It is extremely difficult to accurately date woodenware because its daily use adds years to its appearance in a few months.

Apple knot mallet
C. late nineteenth century.
Value: $55-$65.

This mallet was used for driving wooden pegs into beams in barns.

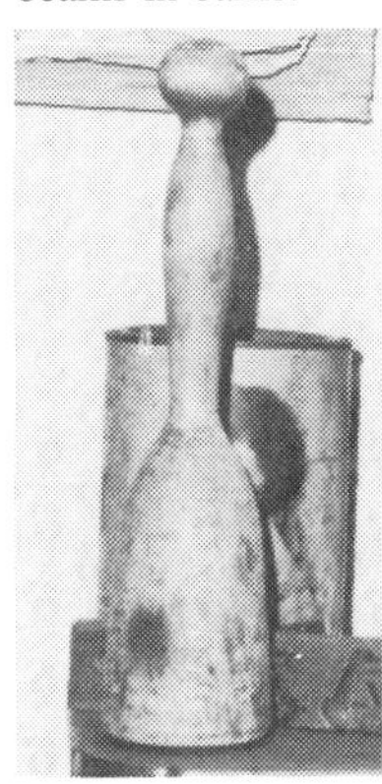

Potato masher
Maple, factory-made, c. 1900.
Value: $15-$20.

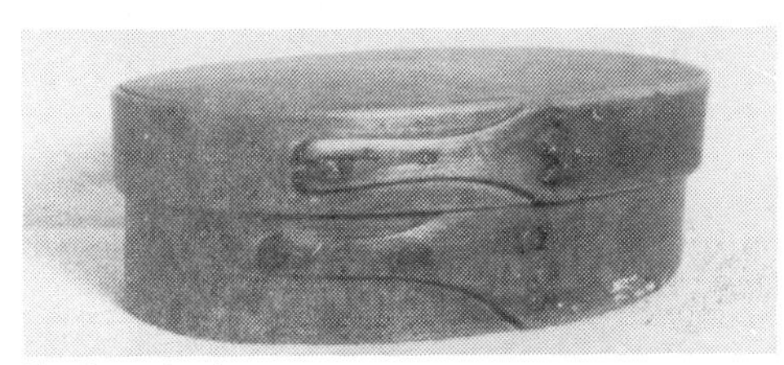

Oval pantry box
Maple sides and pine top, finger lap construction, original finish, c. 1830-1840.
Value: $85-$95.

Compare the finger laps on this colonist or pantry box with several of the Shaker oval boxes in Chapter 7.

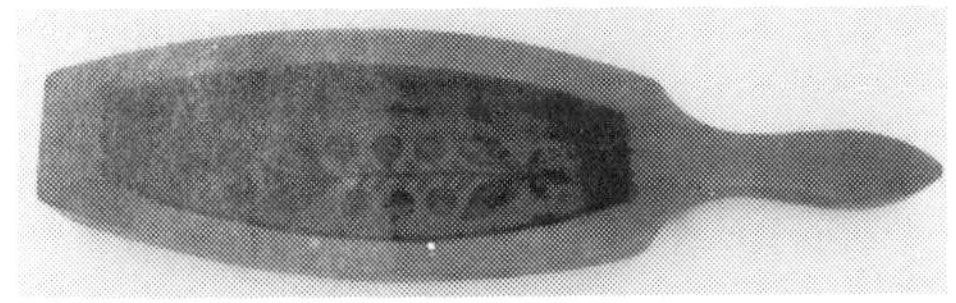

Butterprint
Elongated, handled, cherries and leaves design.
Value: $220-$240.

"Lollipop" butter print
Diameter, 4¼".
Value: $265-$285.

"Double thistle" cup-type butter print
Almost 5" diameter.
Value: $190-$210.

Eight-print mold
Leaf, rosebud, two raspberries, ear of corn, pineapple, grapes, clover, sheaf of wheat, 4½" x 10".
Value: $240-$270.

Cow butter mold
Diameter, 2½".
Value: $170-$190.

Rooster print
Value: $240-$260.

"Lollipop" butter print
Diameter, 4½", 8½" long.
Value: $265-$285.

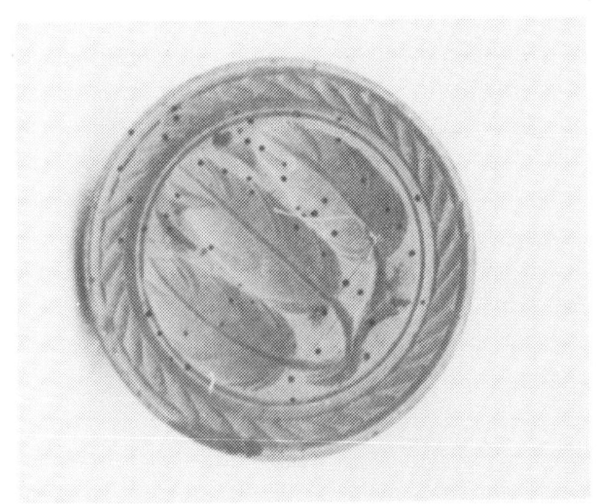

Three leaves butter print
Almost 4″ diameter.
Value: $80-$100.

Swan butter print
Diameter, 4½″.
Value: $165-$185.

Two pears butter print
Almost 4″ diameter.
Value: $160-$180.

Basket with apple and cucumber butter print
Diameter, 4″.
Value: $365-$385.

Six acorns butter print
Diameter, 4″.
Value: $115-$135.

Tulip butter print
Diameter, 4½″.
Value: $265-$285.

Heart butter print
Diameter, 4¼″.
Value: $130-$150.

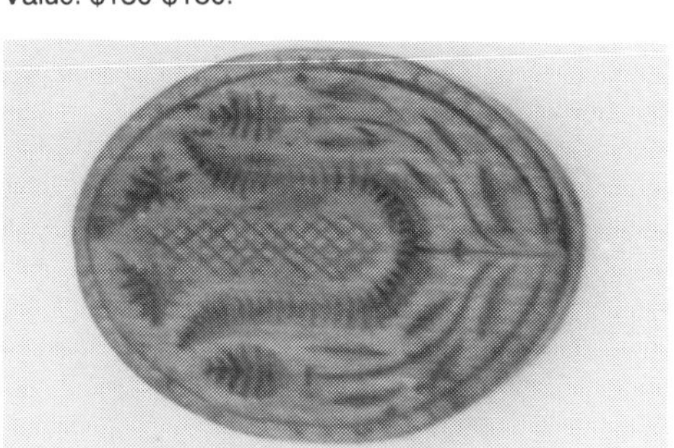

Oval, tulip butter print
Dimensions, 3½″ x 5″.
Value: $240-$260.

Sunflower butter print
Diameter, 4″.
Value: $175.

Four print butter mold
Tree of life, rose, thistle, and circle approximately 5″ x 7″.
Value: $280-$320.

Fish butter mold
Almost 3″ diameter.
Value: $240-$260.

Pennsylvania Dutch pineapple and stars print
Value: $140-$160.

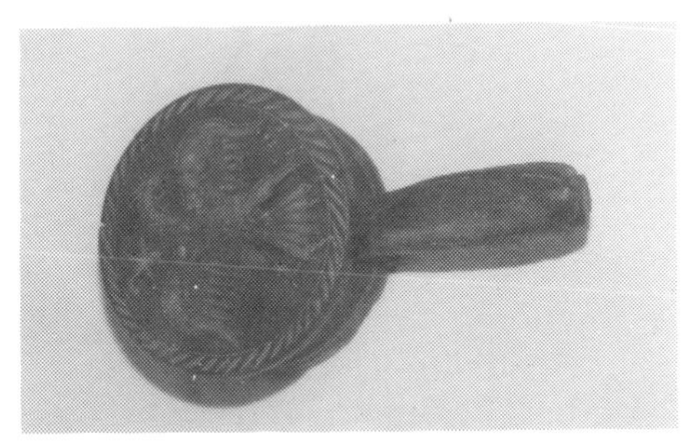

Lollipop double print
Carved heart on one side and American eagle and star on the other.
Value: $425-$475.

Box butter mold with double print
Print of a cow and print of a pineapple.
Value: $250-$275.

Swan butter mold
Value: $180-$195.

Box butter mold
Carved into the surface of the print is "Dairy Queen."
Value: $150-$175.

Carved leaves butter print
Diameter, 3½″.
Value: $90-$95.

Carved leaves, flower, and stars print
Diameter, 4½″.
Value: $150-$175.

Maple sugar heart mold
Hand-carved of pine, late nineteenth century, New England.
Value: $200-$225.

Maple sugar mold
Leaves and flower design.
Value: $200-$225.

Butter mold
Maple, hand-carved leaf design, c. 1850.
Value: $85-$100.

Basket of flowers butter mold
Hand-carved.
Value: $145-$155.

Butter mold
Machine-made cow, maple, c. 1870-1880.
Value: $185-$225.

The value of a butter print or mold is largely determined by the design it carries. Animals and birds are difficult to find and expensive to buy. The more commonly found designs include leaves, flowers, wheat, or geometric patterns.

Butter print
Rare American eagle, maple, machine-carved, c. 1860-1865.
Value: $250-$275.

Butter print
Maple, possibly English, rare "bird" print, c. 1870-1880.
Value: $225-$250.

The prints or stamps were turned on a lathe and the design was pressed into the maple surface by a machine. Prior to the pressing process, the maple was steamed. In recent years, this particular design has been reproduced in large quantities.

Butter mold
Machine-carved leaves and strawberry, maple, c. 1880.
Value: $75-$95.

The wooden mold that shapes the butter is called a bell or beehive. After the butter was packed into the bell, the plunger was pushed and the butter emerged onto a plate with a form and a decorative design.

Butter print
Maple, wheat design, hand-carved, c. 1860.
Value: $85-$100.

Butter mold
Maple, machine-made, floral decoration, rare form, c. 1870-1875.
Value: $225-$250.

Butter print
Maple, machine-made, c. 1875-1880.
Value: $65-$85.

Butter prints are commonly found in wood, although examples in tin, redware, and ironestone are known. The authors have owned a butter mold with a tin bell or beehive and maple plunger and stamp.

Maple butter print
Hand-carved, geometric patterns, figures, and numbers, c. 1840-1850.
Value: $125-$150.

Metal chocolate molds
C. early 1900s.
Value: $35-$45.

Carved heart maple sugar mold
Pine, New England, c. late nineteenth century.
Value: $85-$95.

Cookie mold
Made four cookies, c. mid-nineteenth century.
Value: $125-$135.

Mortar and pestle
Maple, incised lines, original unpainted condition, c. 1850.
Value: $85-$95.

Mortar and pestle
Maple, early green paint, c.
Value: $90-$100.

Mortar and pestle
Original early condition, decorative lines on mortar, c. 1850.
Value: $75-$85.

Mortar and pestle
Deep green paint, maple, c. 1850-1860.
Value: $100-$120.

Mortars and pestles were popular in early kitchens for grinding spices, herbs, and home-produced medicinal compounds. The interior of a mortar should show much wear and signs of heavy use. Many times the mortar and pestle became separated over the years and a substitute pestle was provided.

Mortar and pestle
Maple, decorative lines on mortar and pestle, c. 1850-1860.
Value: $85-$95.

Mortars and pestles
Maple, c. late nineteenth century.
Value: $50-$55.

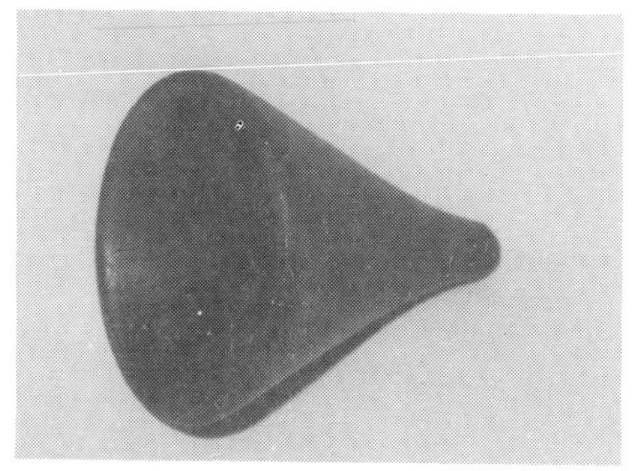

Wooden funnel
Maple, c. late nineteenth century.
Value: $60-$65.

Wooden funnel
Maple, refinished, great early repair on lip, c. 1860.
Value: $80-$90.

Wooden funnel
Maple, original condition, c. 1860.
Value: $80-$90.

Funnels were made of papier-mache, wood, copper, and ironstone.

Staved bucket
Early blue-green paint, button hoops, c. 1850.
Value: $85-$100.

Firkin or sugar bucket
Staved construction, buttonhole hoops, pins, c. 1840, New England, painted red.
Value: $185-$210.

Sugar bucket
Also called a firkin, refinished, staved, swing handle, copper nails and bands, c. 1880.
Value: $85-$100.

Sugar bucket
Ash and maple, staved construction, swing handle, refinished, c. 1880.
Value: $85-$100.

Sugar buckets or firkins in original paint are worth 20 to 40 percent more than the refinished examples.

Lid from sugar bucket
Signed "D. Wilder and Son" from Mass., c. 1880.

This bucket is "signed" only to the extent that the name of the factory in which it was produced is impressed into the lid.

In many antiques shops this adds another 10 to 15 percent to the value. When the term "signed" is used accurately, it normally refers to a signature or wood burn on the bottom of an early Windsor chair.

Miniature firkin
Maple and ash, 6" diameter x 8" high, swing handle, c. 1900-1915.
Value: $65-$75.

Butter tub
Pine, hickory bands, staved construction, c. mid-nineteenth century.
Value: $135-$155.

Painted firkin or sugar bucket
Staved, wooden bands, swing handle, c. 1870.
Value: $90-$110.

Firkin or sugar bucket
Red paint, staved construction, pine, buttonhole hoops, found in New York State, c. 1860.
Value: $150-$175.

Another $10-$15 would be added to the piece if it carried early blue paint rather than red or yellow.

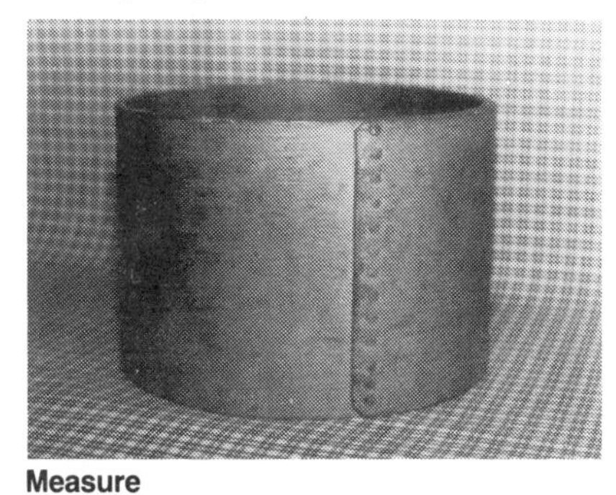

Measure
Painted green, copper nails, maple, late nineteenth century, factory-made.
Value: $25-$30.

This measure was originally sold in a nest of five to eight of varying sizes. In a nest of six measures similar to this example, the value would be $180-$210.

Staved bucket
Buttonhole hoops, pine, painted green, 5½″ high x 6″ diameter, c. 1850.
Value: $145-$155.

Sugar bucket
Staved construction, pine, c. early 1900s, 6½″ high.
Value: $70-$80.

Note the staples that indicate a late, factory-period sugar bucket.

Set of measures
Factory-made, c. 1890-1920.
Value: $60-$75.

Milk bucket
Blue-green paint, Lancaster, Pa., dairy, staved, iron bands, c. early twentieth century.
Value: $70-$75.

Painted bucket
Slaved, red paint, iron bands, 10″ diameter x 6″ high, c. 1860-1870.
Value: $45-$55.

Wooden salt box
Pine staves, hickory bands, red and blue paint, c. 1820-1830.
Value: $200-$225.

A close look at the upper band suggests that it might be an early replacement. Seldom does an early piece make it through 150 years without a legitimate replacement or three.

Early rain barrel
Hand wrought iron bands, 2″ thick pine staves, c. 1830.
Value: $125-$150.

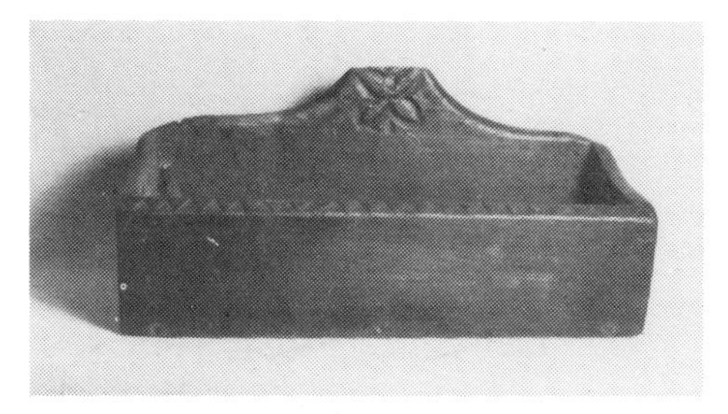

Hanging candle box
Early blue-green paint, pine, c. mid-1800s.
Value: $150-$165.

Knife box
Early green paint, slide top, carved finger pull, c. 1870-1880.
Value: $80-$100.

Turned wooden bowl
Red paint, 4″ diameter, maple, c. 1860.
Value: $50-$75.

Maple spools
Originally from New England textile mills, c. late nineteenth century.
Value: $6-$8 each.

Stack of six cream skimmers
Maple, lathe turned, late nineteenth century.
Value: $25-$40 individually.
$285-$325 as a stack or nest of six.

Turned wooden inkwell
Stenciled decoration, rare form, c, 1830.
Value: $225-$250.

Carved wooden boot inkwell (at left)
Maple, unpainted, c. mid-nineteenth century.
Value: $150-$175.

Slaw cutter
Maple, factory-made, c. 1890-1910.
Value: $28-$32.

Spice chest
Ash, wooden knobs, factory-made, c. 1900.
Value: $65-$75.

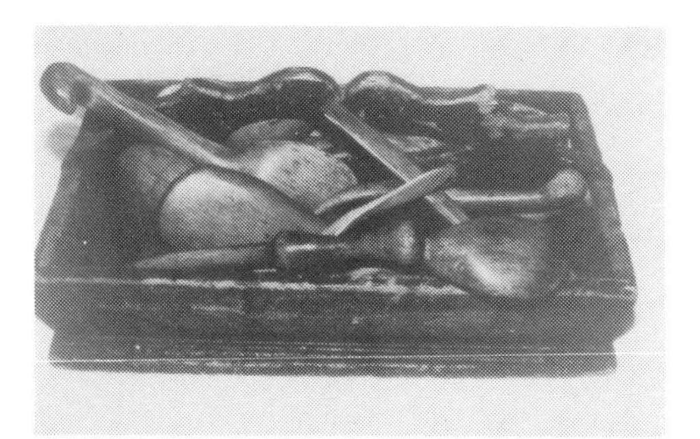

Knife and fork box
Pine, painted a deep red, c. 1860.
Value: $85-$95.

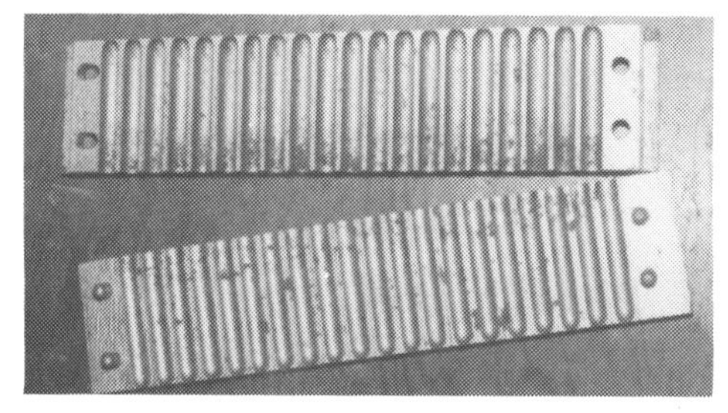

Cigar mold
C. 1890-1915.
Value: $12-$15.

Butter tub
Pine, metal bands, heart handles, c. 1850-1870.
Value: $140-$155.

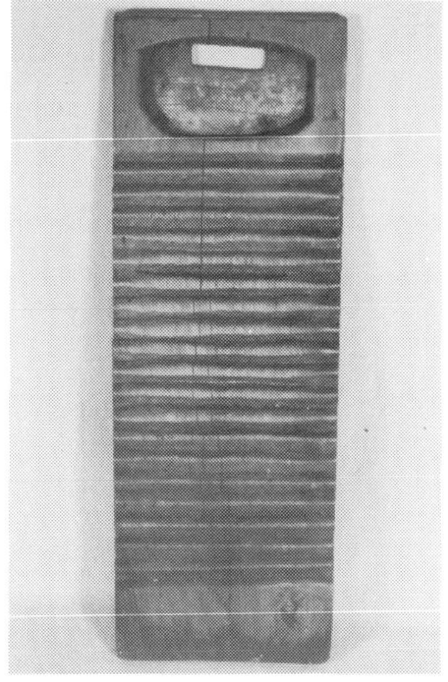

Scrubbing board
Hand hewn, separate area at top for soap, c. 1830.
Value: $140-$150.

Mother Hubbard's patent roller washboard
Pine frame, maple rollers, c. 1920.
Value: $50-$60.

Carved clothespins
C. nineteenth century.
Value: $4-$6 each.

Clothes fork
Used to take clothes from a wash boiler, maple, c. 1890-1900.
Value: $8-$12.

Cross-section of washboards
C. 1840-1920.

Scrub board
Handcrafted, c. 1860.
Value: $85-$100.

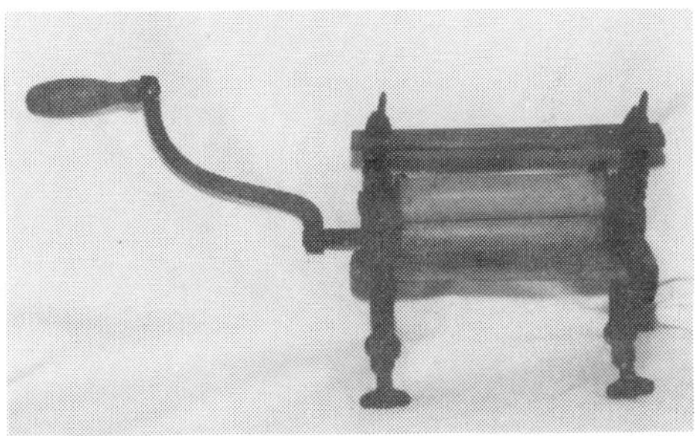

Wringer
C. 1900.
Value: $25-$35.

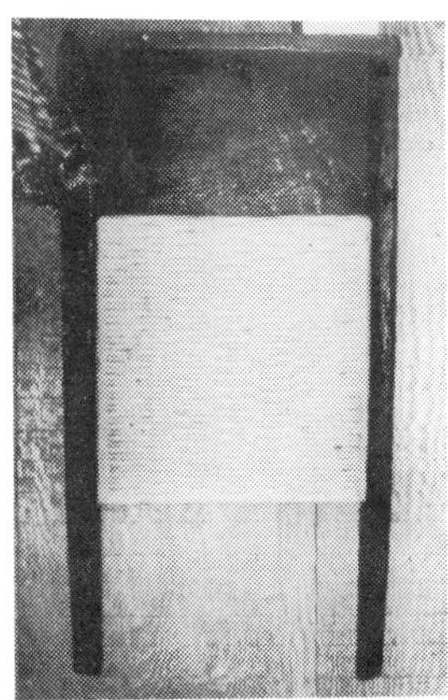

Washboard
C. 1920.
Value: $30-$40.

Child's washday set
C. late nineteenth-early twentieth century.
Value: Bucket - $10-$15.
Tub - $10-$15.
Bench - $10-$15.
Complete set - $75-$95.

NuWash washboard
C. early 1900s.
Value: $55-$65.

Child's tin washboard
C. late nineteenth century - early twentieth century, signed "Sanitary."
Value: $45-$55.

Sad irons
Maple handles, c. 1880s.
Value: $20-$24 each.

Fluting iron (closed)
C. 1890.
Value: $28-$35.

Fluting iron (open)

Washtub
Pine, staved construction, iron bands, piggin handles, c. 1880.
Value: $65-$80.

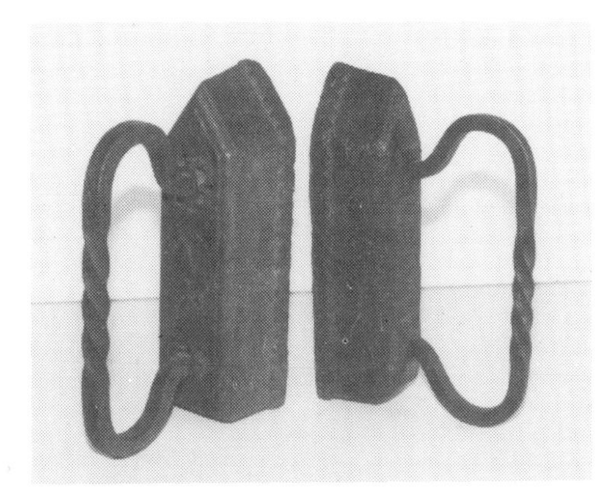

Tailors' irons
Cast iron, c, 1860s.
Value: $45-$55 each.

Fluting iron
C. 1880-1890.
Value: $90-$110.

Fluting iron and irons
C. 1870-1890.
Value: Fluting iron - $45-$55.
Irons - $18-$22.

Child's sewing machine
C. 1880-1900.
Value: $125-$140.

Scrubbing board
Factory-made, child's size, c. 1920-1930.
Value: $35-$45.

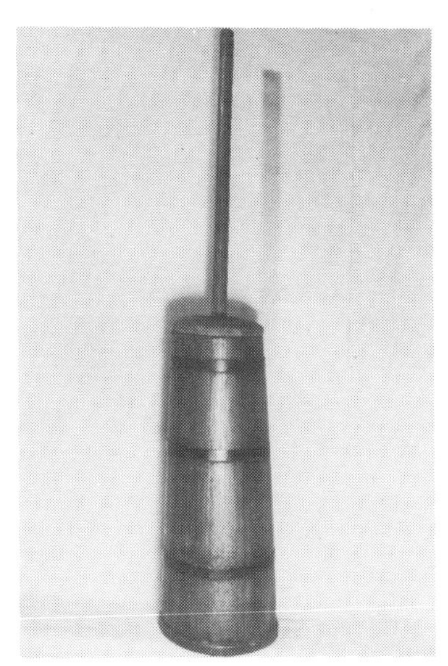

Dasher butter churn
Staved, iron bands, c. 1840.
Value: $225-$250.

Maple bowl
Warped, early green paint, 14½″ diameter, c. 1860.
Value: $100-$125.

Rocking butter churn
Pine, painted red, found in Pennsylvania, c. 1850-1860.
Value: $300-$350.

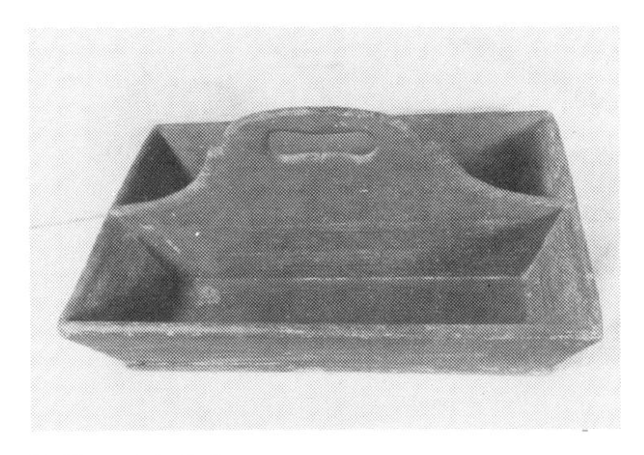

Knife and fork box
Splayed sides, nailed rather than dovetailed, walnut, c. 1860-1870.
Value: $50-$65.

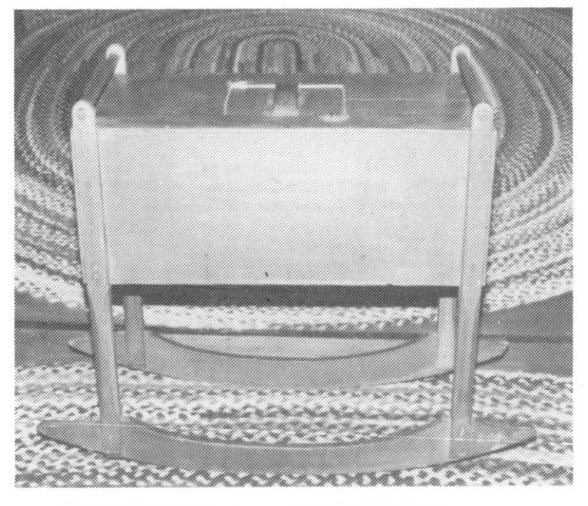

Dasher butter churn
Piggin handle, staved construction, replaced center band, c. 1850.
Value: $140-$150.

Kitchen stool
C. late nineteenth century.
Value: $55-$65.

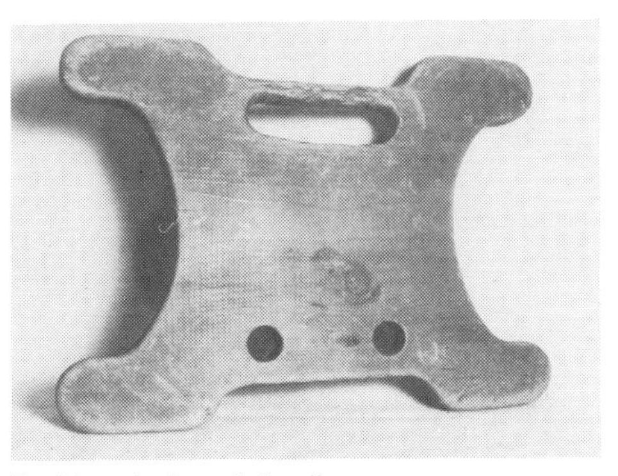

Serving tray
Pine, early paint, probably used in tavern, c. 1840.
Value: $85-$125.

Tool for winding clothesline
Pine, remnants of red paint, c. early twentieth century.
Value: $20-$30.

Wire fly dome and maple chopping board
Both factory-made, domes found in many sizes, c. 1900.
Value: Dome $20-$30 Chopping board: $25-$45.

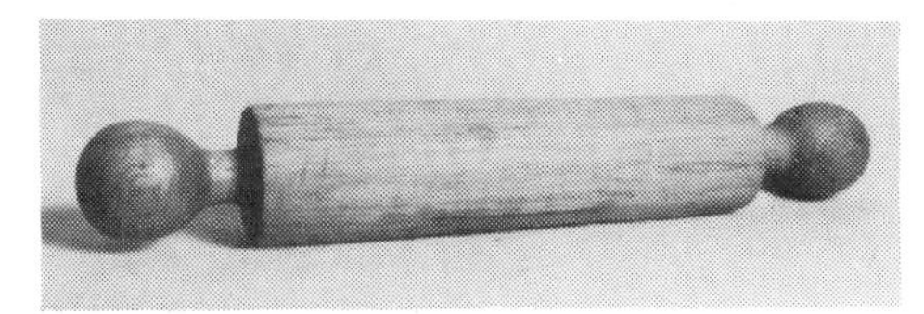

Rolling pin
Maple, factory-made, c. 1900-1920.
Value: $25-$35.

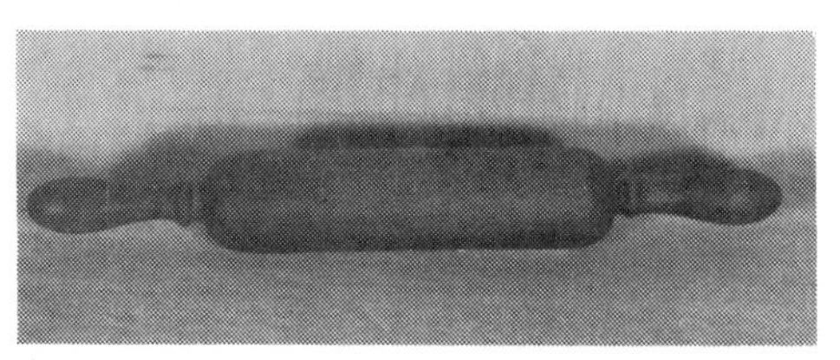

Rolling pin
Maple, factory-made, c. 1880-1890.
Value: $25-$35.

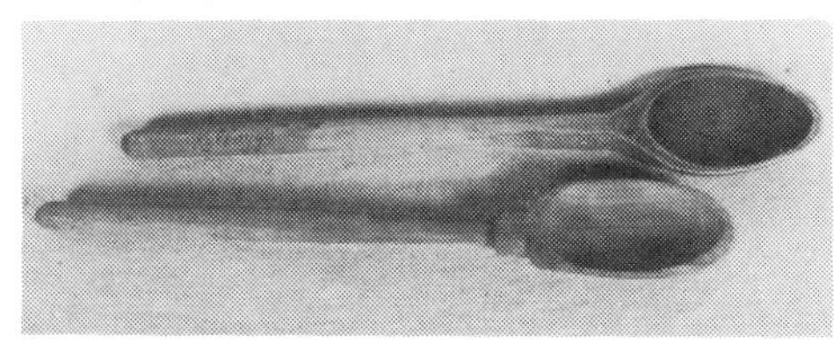

Kitchen spoons
Maple, factory-made, c. 1920-1930.
Value: $6-$8.

Factory-made spoons were manufactured over a long period of time and changed little in design. These spoons are common and may be purchased for a few dollars in most areas. Heavy use in a kitchen can make new woodenware appear old in a few months.

Wooden spoon
Maple, hand-carved, refinished, c. 1880-1900.
Value: $30-$50.

Wooden scoop
Maple, hand-carved, "as found" condition, c. 1860.
Value: $50-$55.

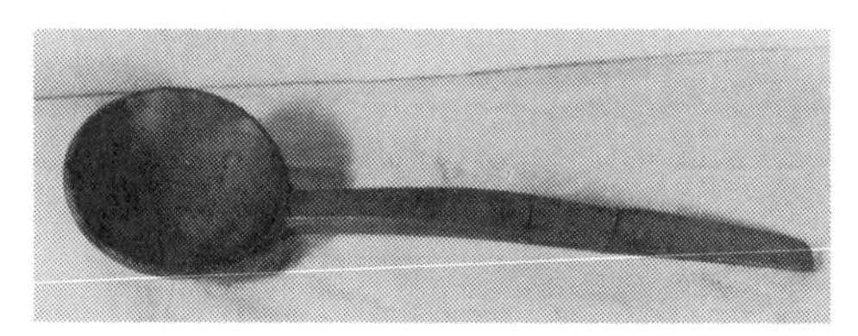

Wooden spoon or ladle
Maple, hand-carved, refinished, c. 1860.
Value: $40-$45.

Wooden spoon or ladle
Maple, hand-carved, c. 1860.
Value: $40-$45.

Pestle and small spoon
Maple, hand-carved spoon possibly European, c. 1850.
Value: Pestle - $18-$25.
Spoon: $35-$45.

It is essential that the collector of woodenware be aware of the imported pieces that are being sold. Some of it appears to be very early and offered at bargain prices.

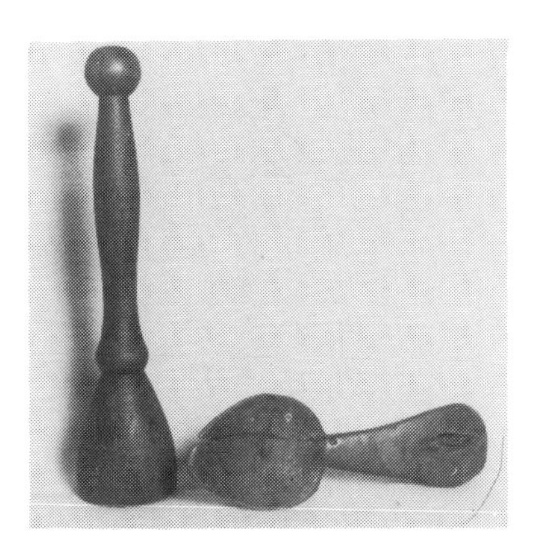

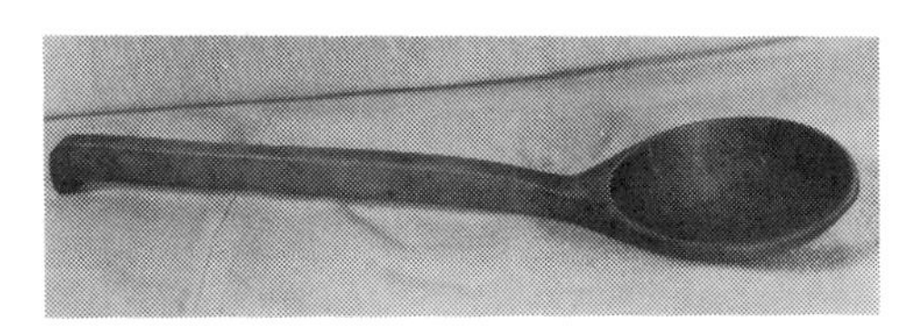

Wooden spoon or ladle
Maple, factory-made, c. 1880.
Value: $15-$20.

Mirror
Early glass, maple frame, 4″ x 4″, c. 1830.
Value: $40-$50.

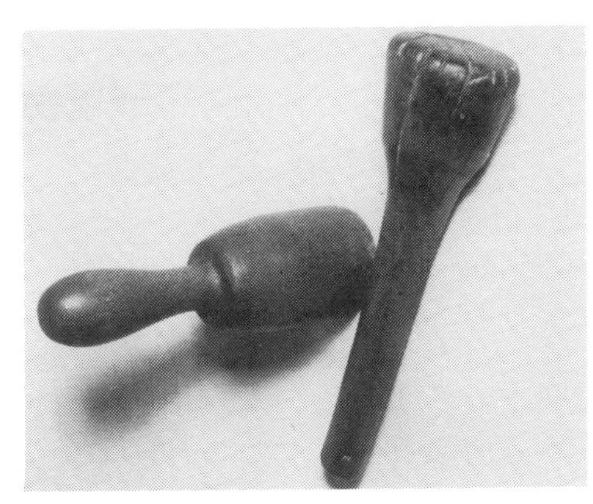

Early pestles
Interesting comparison between the lathe-turned and the hand-carved, c. 1850-1860.
Value: $18-$25.

Footstool
Pine, half-moon legs, mortised construction, early paint, c. 1840.
Value: $45-$55.

Make a special note to study the construction technique used to fasten the top of the stool to the legs. This is an excellent example of the mortise-and-tenon.

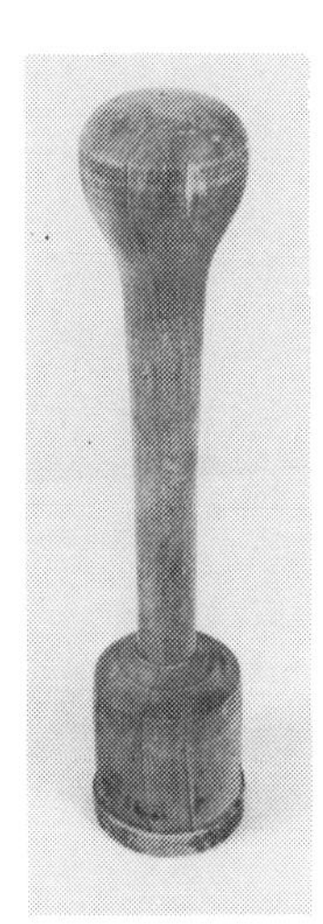

Pestle and meat pounder
Factory-made, maple, found in New York State, c.
Value: $25-$35.

Footstool
Walnut, refinished, found in Amana, Iowa, c. 1870.
Value: $60-$75.

Green bean slicer (back)
Pine, green paint, tin, from Michigan, c. early twentieth century.
Value: $50-$60.

Green bean slicer (front)

Lap desk
Walnut, compartmentalized, original condition, c. 1840-1845.
Value: $85-$110.

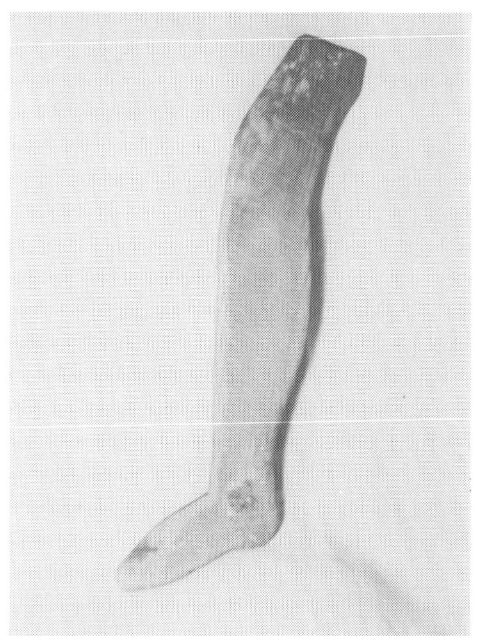

Sock stretcher
Pine, hand-carved, c. 1900.
Value: $25-$40.

Egg box
c. 1930.
Value: $50-$65.

Hay fork
Maple, refinished, factory-made, c. 1890.
Value: $100-$125.

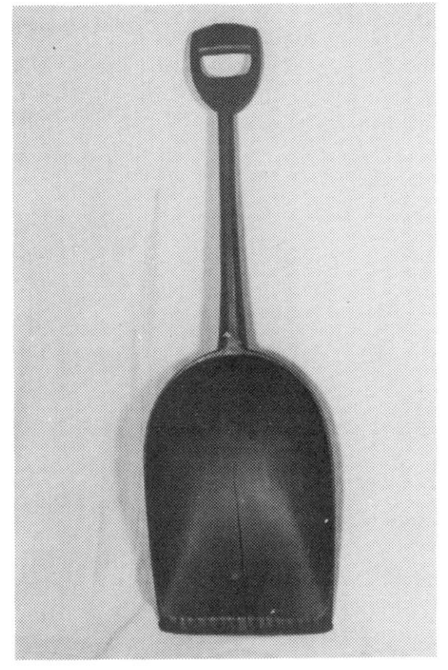

Grain shovel
Worn red paint, maple, early repair to crack at base of scoop, c. 1860-1870.
Value: $135-$150.

Tin cookie cutter
French, from commercial bakery, 20″ high, c. early twentieth century.
Value: $225-$275.

Tin cookie cutter and tin rolling pin
Maple handles on rolling pin, c. late nineteenth century.
Value: Cookie cutter - $40-$50.
Rolling pin - $45-$60.

Tin kitchen utensils and cookie cutters are still relatively inexpensive. There is no question that in the near future tin items will appreciate significantly in demand and price. The rolling pin originally was sold with a rectangular tin sheet for rolling dough. The sheet was designed to hang on the wall and had a tray at its base for the rolling pin. If the set were together, the value of the pin and tray would be $95-$120.

Cookie cutters
Tin, strap handles on back, found in eastern Indiana, c. 1870-1900.
Value: Man $25-$35.
Woman - $40-$50.

Strainer
Tin, probably made and sold by a traveling tinsmith, c. 1860-1870.
Value: $30-$35.

Cookie cutter
Tin, later form, c. early twentieth century.
Value: $8-$12.

Tin container
Small ring handle, c. 1900.
Value: $20-$25.

Measure
Tin, probably one of a set of three to six, c. 1860.
Value: $12-$18.

Double foot stove
Maple frame, pierced tin top and sides, bail handle, c. 1830.
Value: $225-$245.

This foot stove contains two small tin buckets for hot coals. Double stoves are much less common than the smaller foot stoves. A conventional foot stove should sell for $100-$120, depending upon its condition.

Tin pastry cutter and tin raisin container
C. late 19th century - cutter; c. 1915-1925 - container.
Value: $25-$35 - cutter
$25-$30 - container

Tin kitchen utensils
C. early 1900s.
Values: Heart cookie cutter — $14-$18.
Candy mold — $10-$12.
Scoop — $4-$6.

Tin scoops and cookie cutter
C. early 1900s.
Value: Scoop with handle — $10-$12.
Flour or sugar scoop — $6-$8.
Cookie cutter — $12-$14.

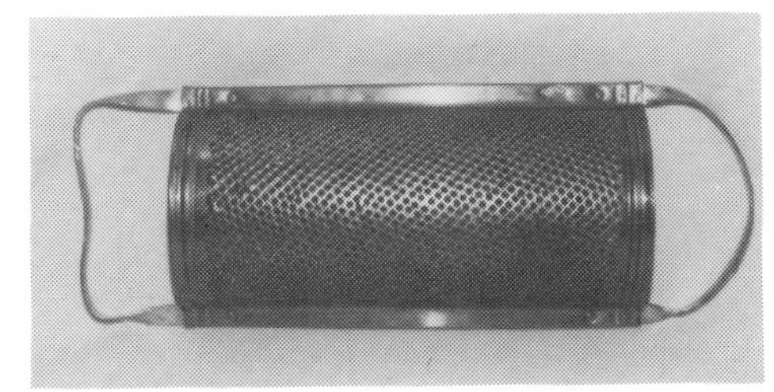

Food grater
C. 1930s.
Value: $3-$5.

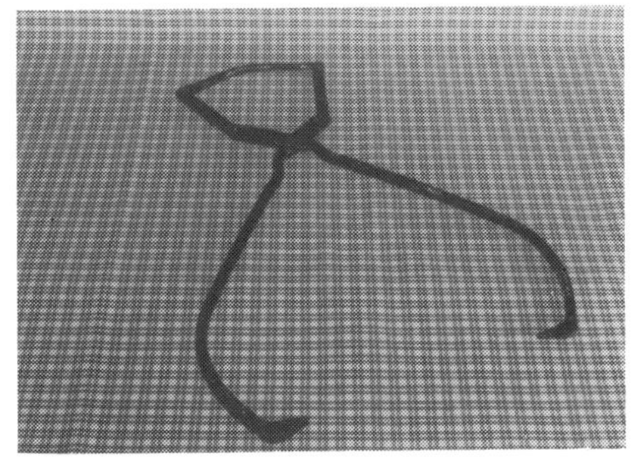

Ice tongs
C. 1920-1930.
Value: $18-$22.

String holder
Cast iron, c. 1930.
Value: $20-$24.

Ice cream scoop
C. 1930.
Value: $12-$14.

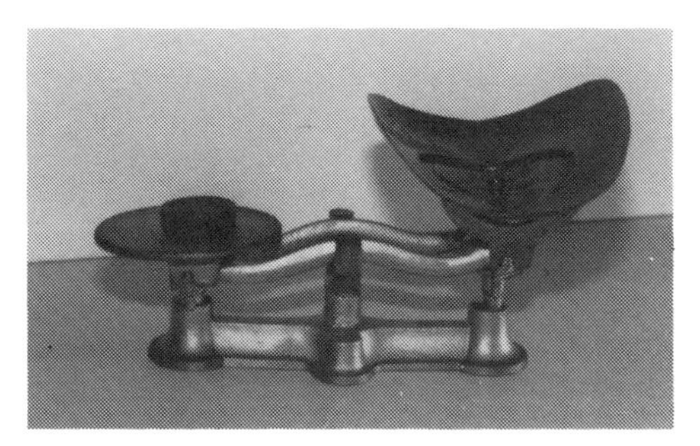

Iron scales
Tin scoop, c. 1900.
Value: $35-$50.

Spice box
Tin, six drawers and storage area above, c. 1870-1900.
Value: $95-$125.

Chopping knife and dough scraper
Maple handle and steel blade, wrought iron dough scraper, c. 1900; chopping knife, c. 1840.
Value: Chopping knife — $35-$45.
Dough scraper — $25-$30.

Dough scrapers were used to recapture bits of dough stuck to the bottoms of bowls or table tops.

Iron scales
Brass scoop, weights with ring handles, c. 1870s.
Value: $160-$190.

Chopping knife
C. 1880-1900.
Value: $25.-$35.

Chopping knife,
Earlier form, iron blade, maple handle, c. 1850.
Value: $30-$40.

Chopping knife
C. 1880.
Value: $25-$30.

Late chopping knife
Maple handle, steel blade, c. 1920.
Value: $20-$25.

Coffee grinder
Factory-made, c. 1880-1910.
Value: $65-$95.

Coffee grinder
Factory-made, early 1900s, refinished, possibly European.
Value: $65-$75.

Crystal coffee grinder
C. 1920, cast iron base.
Value: $75-$85.

Enterprise coffee grinder
Model #5, original paint and stenciling, early replacement drawer, c. late nineteenth century.
Value: $250-$275.

Canister coffee grinder or mill
Made for hanging on wall, used in the home, c. 1890-1910.
Value: $70-$85.

The early mail order houses sold thousands of these grinders to turn-of-the-century coffee drinkers.

Bell corn grinder
Original black and red paint, c. 1890.
Value: $45-$55.

It is not uncommon for collectors to hear their hearts pounding when they happen upon a wheeled grinder in old paint with a $30 price tag. Unfortunately, the bargain turns out to be a grinder used to grind corn rather than coffee.

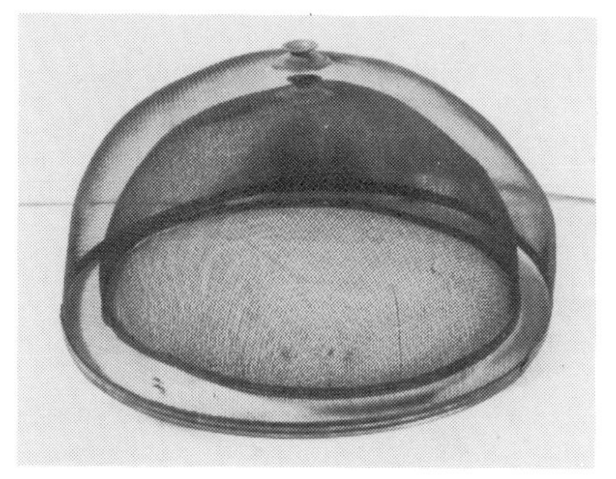

Fly dome
Wire, maple, "knob" handle, c. 1880.
Value: $25-$35.

Flies were a major irritant in late nineteenth century kitchens. Fly domes were found in a variety of sizes and were placed over plates of baked goods or food to keep the flies away. The smaller domes are less commonly found than the larger ones.

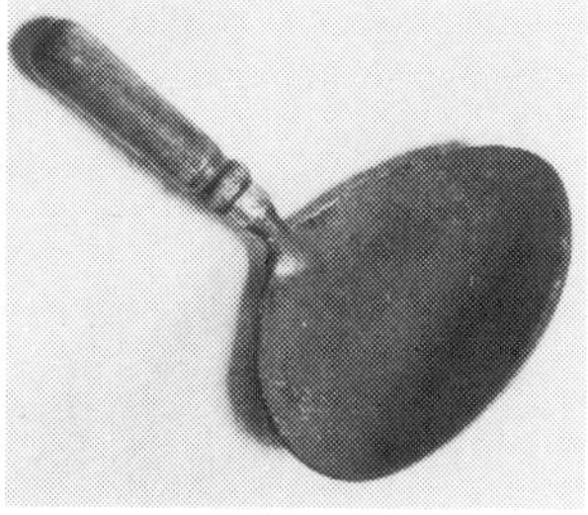

Iron ladle
Maple handle, early factory-made, c. 1860-1870.
Value: $35-$50.

Fresh Eggs sign
Black letters on white background, tin, c. early twentieth century.
Value: $50-$60.

Apple butter kettle
Copper, iron bail handle, dovetailed side and bottom, 36″ diameter, c. 1870-1880.
Value: $275-$325.

In the 1960s, a trip into the apple country of southern Illinois could net at least one kettle in every antiques shop.

The kettles were heavily covered with carbon and required dedication or a professional to clean. The kettles have almost vanished at this point to the sides of fireplaces throughout the Middle West.

Copper kettle
Diameter 32″, c. 1880s, burnished.
Value: $350-$450.

Brass kettle
Diameter 14″, used in making jams and jellies, burnished, c. 1880-1900.
Value: $120-$135.

Brass kettle
Diameter 11″, c. 1880-1900.
Value: $95-$115.

Copper teakettle
"Gooseneck," dovetailed bottom, c. 1840-1860.
Value: $185-$225.

Copper teakettle
Originally nickle-plated, c. 1900-1925, burnished.
Value: $45-$55.

Copper teakettle
Dovetailed bottom, swing handle, c. 1820-1840.
Value: $200-$235.

Copper coffeepot
Originally nickel-plated, c. 1910.
Value: $65-$75.

Copper coffeepot
Maple handle, c. 1900-1925, burnished.
Value: $55-$65.

Brass scoop from set of scales
Burnished, 13″ long x 6½″ wide, c. 1900.
Value: $55-$65.

Milk scale
Brass, 5½″ diameter.
Value: $30-$35.

School bell
Brass, 5½″ diameter.
Value: $50-$55.

Iron hearth trivet
Handwrought,
c. 1840.
Value: $65-$75.

Metal teakettle
Unmarked,
c. 1850-1860.
Value: $115-$130.

Copper pudding molds
Tin-lined, c. 1870-1900.
Value: $75-$85 each.

Pewter charger
Marked Flagg and Homan, 1840.
Value: $425-$475.

Iron kettle
"Goose neck" spout, bail handle, New York State, c. 1840.
Value: $100-$125.

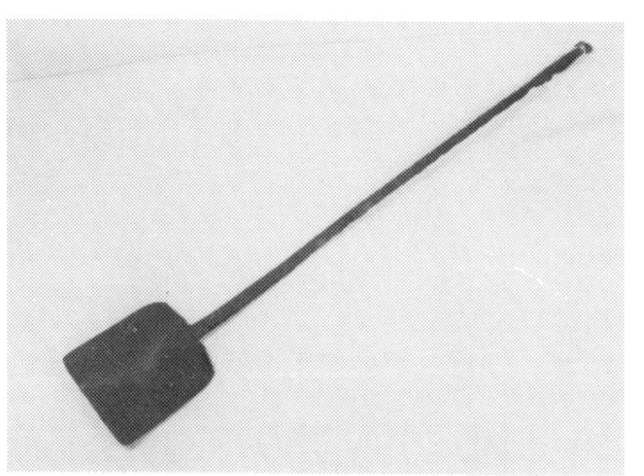

Peel
Iron, hand forged, used to remove bread from a bake oven, c. 1820-1830.
Value: $70-$85.

Sugar nippers
Hand forged, designed for table use, c. 1780-1800.
Value: $85-$100.

Sugar nippers were used to cut the cones of sugar that were in use during the colonial period. This example was used at the table and passed from diner to diner as the need arose.

Porringer
Iron, cast in an early mold, c. 1800.
Value: $80-$90.

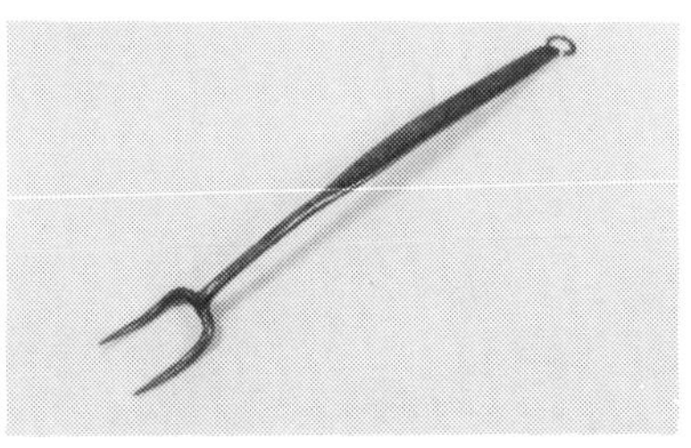

Toasting fork
Hand forged iron, c. early nineteenth century.
Value: $60.-$70.

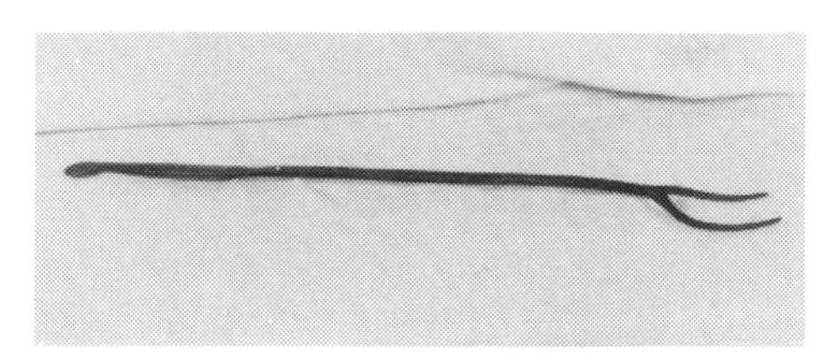

Toasting fork
Hand forged iron, c. early nineteenth century.
Value: $65-$75.

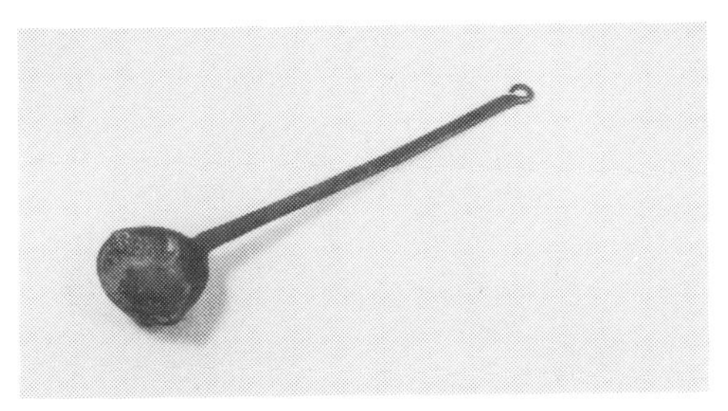

Ladle
"Rattail" hanging hook, c. 1840.
Value: $45-$60.

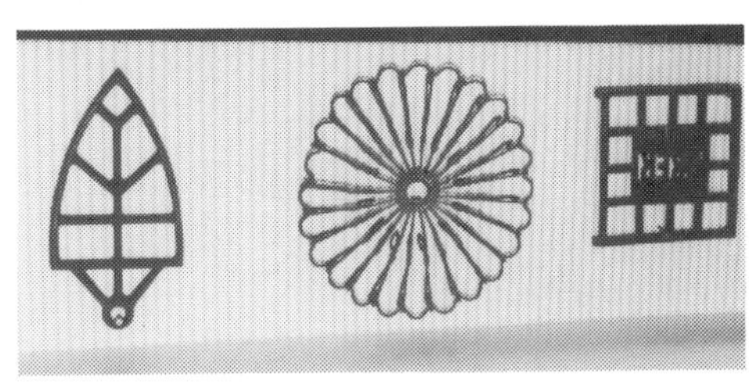

Trivets
C. 1900-1920.
Values: Square iron trivet — $22-$28.
Wire trivet — $18-$22.
Iron trivet — $18-$22.

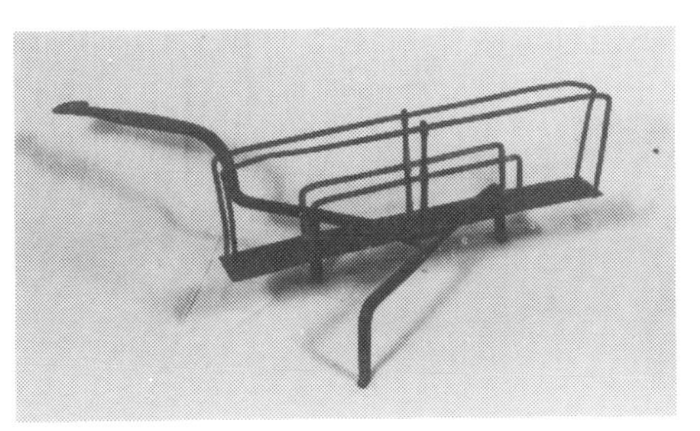

Iron toaster
Rotating toaster, three legs, hand-forged, c. 1830.
Value: $175-$200.

Iron trivets
C. late nineteenth century.
Value: $24-$32.

Cast iron trivet
C. 1870.
Value: $24-$28.

Cast iron trivet
C. 1880-1890.
Value: $45-$55.

Pie crimper
C. 1830-1840.
Value: $60-$70.

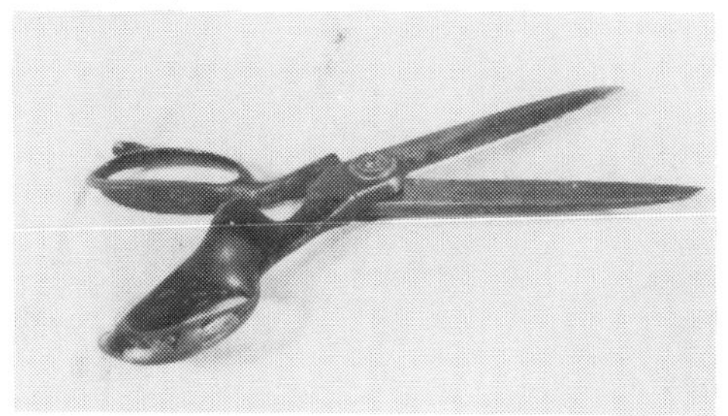

Tailor's scissors
C. 1880.
Value: $20-$30.

Scales
C. late nineteenth century.
Value: $35.-$45.

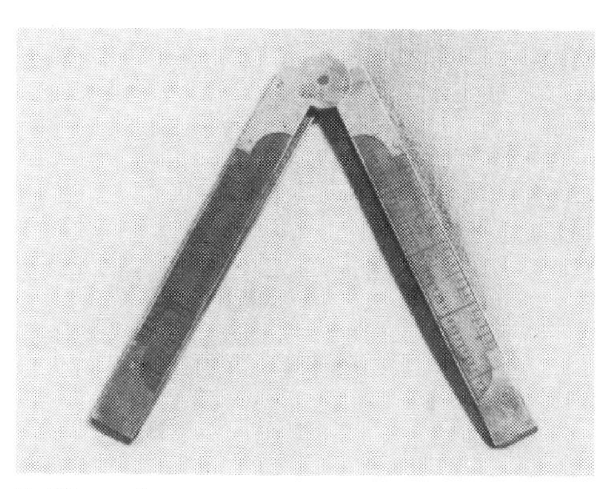

Folding ruler
Brass and maple, c. 1880.
Value: $25-$30.

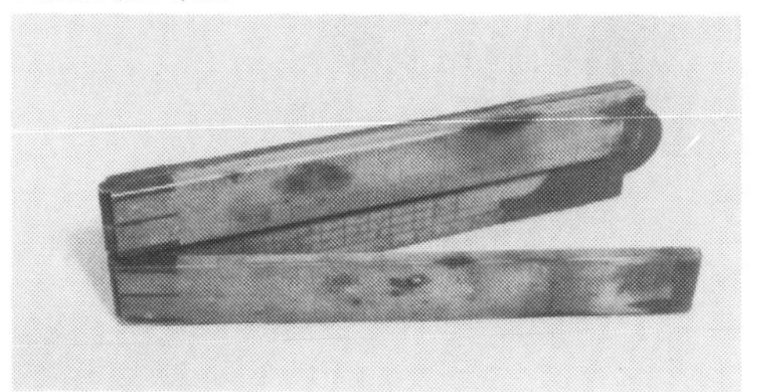

Folding ruler
Brass and maple, c. 1880.
Value: $25-$30.

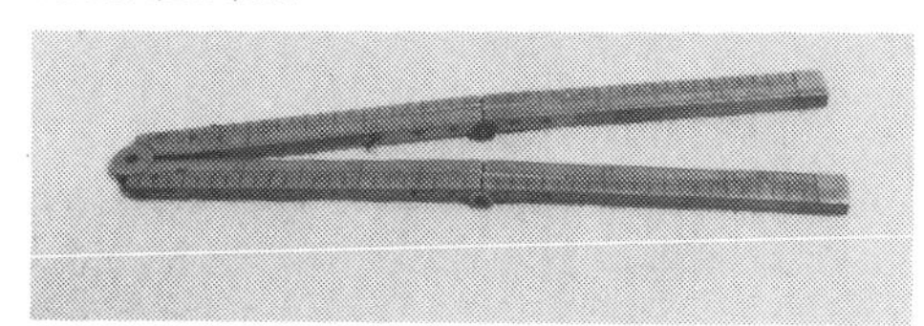

Folding ruler
Brass and maple, c. 1880.
Value: $25-$30.

Vaporizer
Tin, early one for home use, c. 1890-1900.
Value: $35-$45.

The screw cap was removed and water was placed in the upper portion of the vaporizer. In the open area below, a small candle provided enough heat to produce a minimal amount of steam.

Tea and coffee canisters
Unmarked, stenciled decoration, probably given as a premium, c. 1880-1900.
Value: $50-$60.

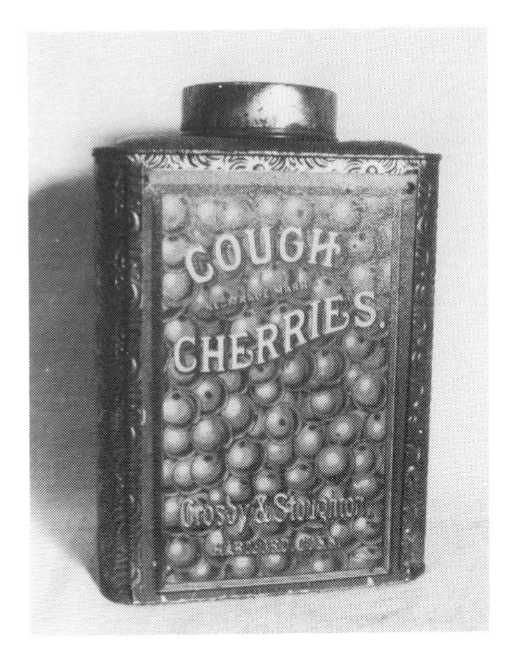

Cough cherries container
For store use, slide-out label allowed other items to be stored in the same container with a new label, c. 1890.
Value, $85-$110.

Tobacco tin
Central Union Cut Plug, "lunchbox"-type, tin, c. 1885.
Value: $65-$75.

Peanut butter tin
Bail handle, c. 1920.
Value: $45-$55.

Cereal tin
"Grape Nuts," black and yellow decoration, c. 1900.
Value: $75-$95.

Candy container
"Dixie Queen" stick candy, c. 1930.
Value: $25-$30.

Variety of home remedy bottles
C. late 1800s-early 1900s.
Value: $10-$40.

In the late 1960s, a large number of Oceanic Cut Plug and Dan Patch Cut Plug tins were found in a Detroit warehouse and offered by an Ohio dealer in the *Antique Trader*. The tins were priced at less than $10 and were in mint condition.

Tobacco and food tins
C. late 1800s-early 1900s.
Value: $25-$65.

Flour container
C. 1880.
Value: $65-$75.

Wafer tin
C. 1940.
Value: $20-$25.

Mustard plaster tin
C. 1930.
Value: $10-$15.

Coffee tin
C. 1930s.
Value: $20-$24.

Quaker Oats boxes
C. 1930s.
Value: $7-$9 each.

Soap packages
C. 1920-1930.
Value: $4-$5 each.

Cleaning packages
C. 1910-1920.
Value: $3-$6 each.

Oval cake mold
Cast iron, New York State, c. 1820-1830.
Value: $75-$100.

"Turk's Turban" cake mold
Cast iron, New York State, c. 1870.
Value: $50-$60.

Cake mold
Cast iron, c. 1880-1900.
Value: $45-$55.

Cornbread mold
Cast iron, c. 1890s.
Value: $16-$20.

Fire bucket
"Sand for Fire Only" — stenciled, c. 1880.
Value: $75-$90.

Frypan
Cast iron, found in West Virginia, c. early twentieth century.
Value: $25-$30.

Iron pot
Bail handle, three iron legs, c. 1890.
Value: $50-$65.

Iron pot
Bail handle, three raised legs, possibly European, c. 1850.
Value: $60-$75.

Kettle
Cast iron, c. late nineteenth century
Value: $45-$55.

Meat hook
Iron, c. 1930s.
Value: $12-$16.

Coal bucket
Metal, painted black, c. 1920s.
Value: $15-$18.

Cross-section of kitchen collectibles
From the 1900-1930 period.

Fire bucket
Leather, painted green with gold lettering, c. 1830-1840.
Value: $275-$300.

Canister set
C. 1940.
Value: $18-$25.

Advertising card
KC Baking Powder, c. 1930.
Value: $1.

Paper lids for milk and cream bottles
C. 1930s, Honegger Dairy, Forrest, Illinois.
Value: $.40-$.60 (cents).

Any price guide must have a range of items that are evaluated. It might be a world's record to include something worth .40 cents to .60 cents but it illustrates a point. If your name is Honegger and your family owned a dairy that has since closed, you would pay a great deal for family mementoes. Thus, the emotional or sentimental aspect of a given item may cloud your judgment when buying or selling it. When finding and buying antiques, it is extremely difficult to maintain even a modicum of objectivity.

Straw container, scale, ice tongs
C. 1920-1940.
Value: Straw container — $14-$20.
Scale — $12-$16.
Ice tongs — $8-$12.

Glass counter display jars
C. 1900-1920.
Value: $20-$25.

Tin canister set
C. 1920.
Value: $40-$45.

Milk and cream bottles
C. 1930.
Value: $6-$8.

Dazey butter churn
C. 1920.
Value: $40-$50.

Rolling pins and turn-of-the-century tin utensils
Value: Flour sack — $8-$12.
Flour sifter — $6-$8.
Muffin tin — $3-$4.
Metal scoop — $3-$4.
Cookie cutter — $2-$3.
Tin measure — $2-$4.

Graniteware pots and kettles
C. 1930s.
Values: $6-$20.

Grocery sack
Forrest, Illinois, c. 1930.
Value: $.50 (cents).

If you bought penny candy or *Superman No. 1* at the Main Street Market or if your telephone number was 34, this sack might even be worth one dollar.

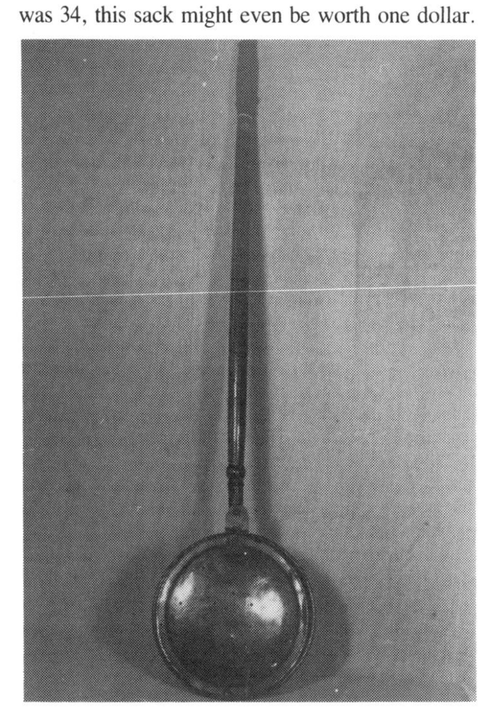

Copper warming pan
Incised decoration on lid, found in Pennsylvania, c. 1830.
Value: $250-$275.

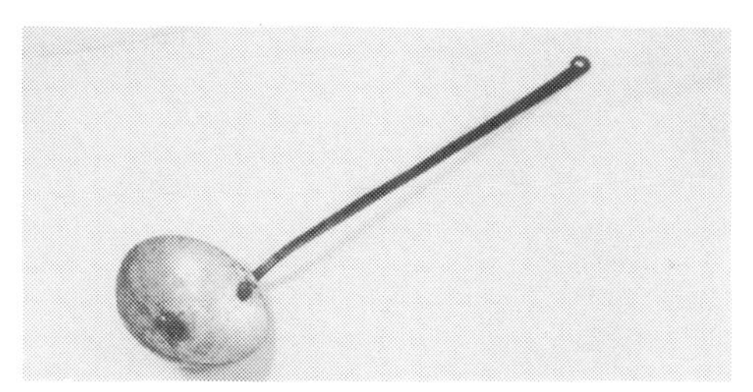

Iron and brass ladle
C. 1830.
Value: $85-$95.

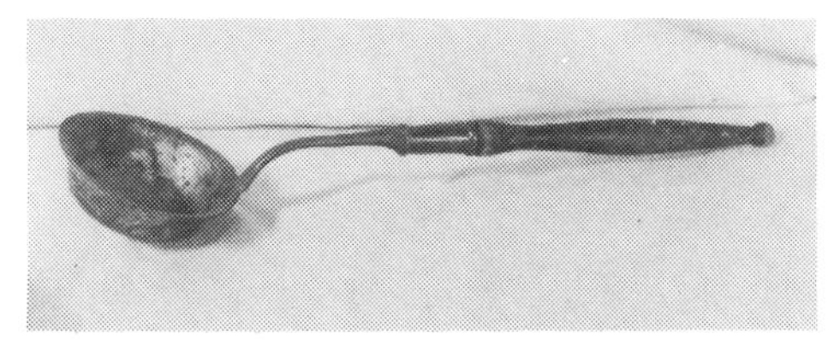

Pewter ladle with turned wood handle
C. 1820.
Value: $125-$150.

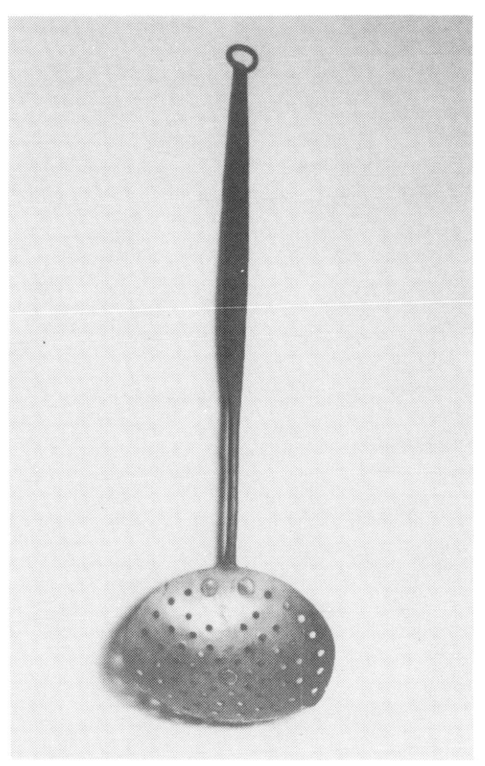

Brass skimmer
Iron handle, copper nails, Pennsylvania, c. 1840.
Value: $100-$125.

Brass skimmer with iron handle
C. 1820.
Value: $100-$125.

Brass ladle with iron handle
Probably European, copper patches, c. nineteenth century.
Value: $65-$75.

Compare the workmanship of this ladle and the example at left to the other skimmers and ladles. The workmanship is obviously inferior to the American utensils.

Copper ladle with iron handle
Probably European, c. nineteenth century.
Value: $55-$60.

This is another example of an imported kitchen utensil that is sold as American-made. It is also crudely constructed when it is compared with American craftsmanship.

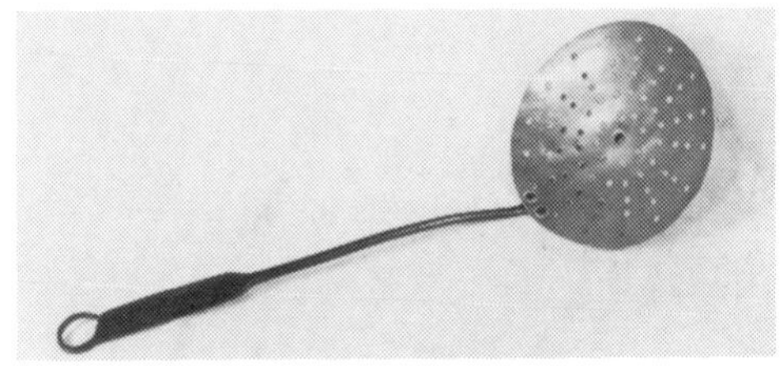

Brass skimmer with iron handle
C. 1830.
Value: $90-$115.

Brass kitchen scoop
C. 1890.
Value: $30-$45.

Cottage cheese drainer
Tin, bow handles, New York State, c. 1850-1860.
Value: $65-$75.

Wall clock
Made in Waterbury, Connecticut, key wound mechanism, c. 1880-1890.
Value: $130-$140.

Iron trivet and pewter candlestick
c. 1840.
Value: Trivet — $50-$75.
Candlestick — $85-$100.

The trivet is similar to many that have been imported in the past decade from Europe. The unmarked candlestick is English and dates from the mid-1800s.

High scraper candlestick
Iron, c. 1840-1850.
Value: $55-$65.

Tin candleholder
C. 1850.
Value: $60-$70.

Tin candleholder
Finger hold, slide tab to regulate candle height, c. 1850.
Value: $65-$75.

Tin candleholder
Designed to be stuck in a beam or small opening, c. 1830.
Value: $45-$55.

Tin candleholder
Saucer base, finger hold, tab to adjust candle height, c. 1840.
Value: $75-$100.

Iron candleholder
Hog-scraper type, tab to adjust candle height, c. 1840.
Value: $80-$110.

Pair of Queen Anne candlesticks
Cast brass, English, c. 1750.
Value: $180-$200.

Hog-scraper candlesticks are similar in design to a common Midwestern tool that was used to scrape bristles from hogs at butchering time each fall. A hog scraper has a wooden handle and an iron base.

The rarest hog-scraper candlestick has a brass ring around the center of the shaft. A hog-scraper with a "wedding ring" on its shaft is worth at least $200-$275.

Saucer candleholder
Tin, finger hold, c. 1975.
Value: $18-$20.

This is a reproduction that was allowed to sit in the rain and snow for a winter and emerged as a century-old rarity. The uninitiated would stand in line to purchase a similar piece for $95-$125.

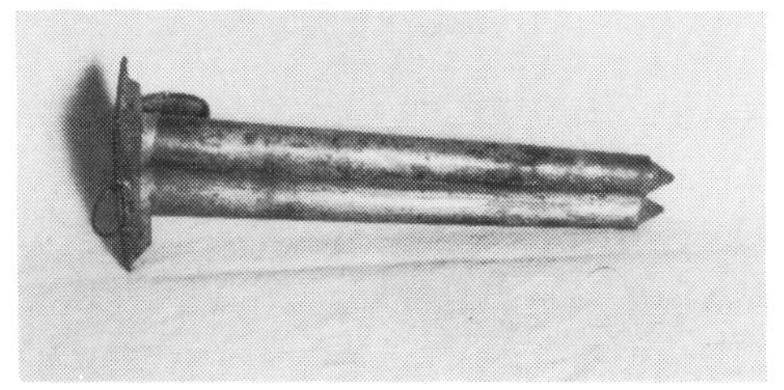

Tin candle mold
Two-tube, strap handle, hanging ring, c. 1840.
Value: $65-$75.

Tin candle mold
Strap handle, miniature, for making Christmas tree candles, twelve tubes, c. 1850.
Value: $300-$350.

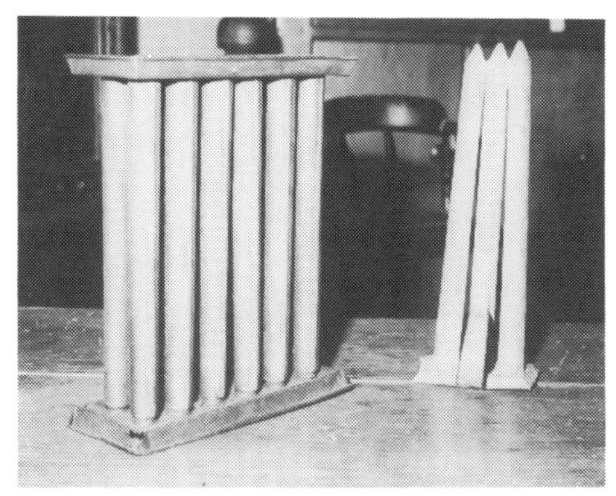

Tin candle molds
Twelve-tube, hanging three-tube mold, c. 1850.
Value: Twelve-tube mold — $75-$100.
Three-tube mold — $60-$85.

Tin candle mold
Eighteen-tube, two strap handles, c. 1850.
Value: $110-$125.

Tin candle mold
Four-tube, hanging, strap handle, c. 1850.
Value: $80-$95.

Tin candle mold
Four-tube standing mold, strap handle, c. 1850.
Value: $80-$95.

Tin candle mold
Six-tube standing mold, strap handle, c. 1850.
Value: $90-$100.

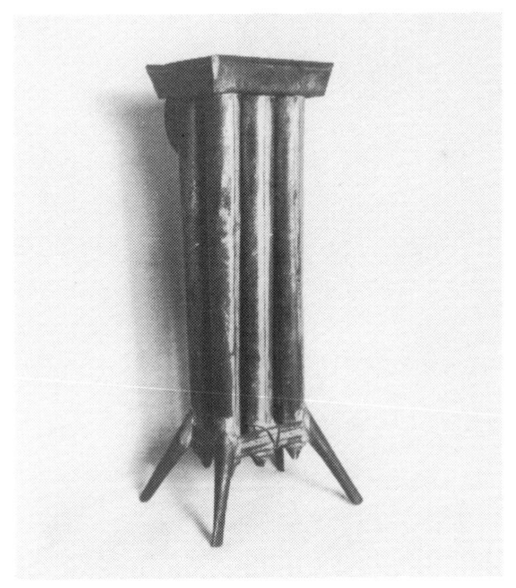

Tin candle mold
Six-tube, on four splayed legs, c. 1850.
Value: $175-$200.

Pierced tin candle lantern
Original early condition, called "Paul Revere" lantern, c. 1840.
Value: $175-$200.

These have been reproduced since the early 1900s, and many early reproductions now carry all the attributes of distinguished old age.

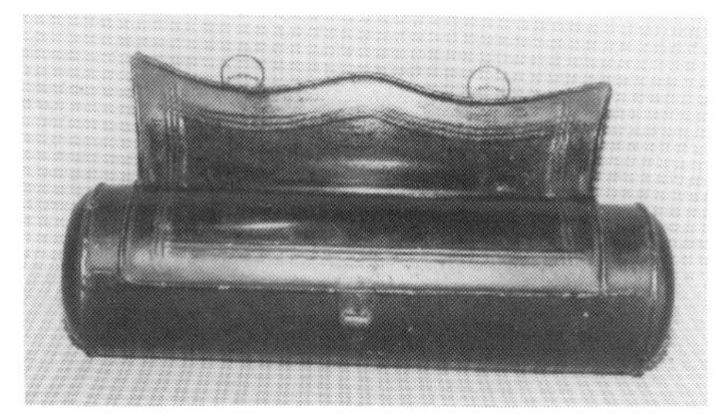

Candle box
Tin, painted black, c. 1850-1860.
Value: $225-$240.

Candle dip
Pine, painted red, wire hooks, c. 1840.
Value: $125-$145.

Lantern
Iron, New England, c. 1840-1860.
Value: $275-$325.

Table lantern
Glazed sides, walnut, Pennsylvania, c. 1830.
Value: $250-$350.

Kerosene lantern
Metal, painted black, c. early 1900s.
Value: $75-$95.

Compare the designs punched into the tin. The tin was stamped rather than hand pierced in a random fashion. Lamps of this type have often lost their oil burner and been replaced with a "make-do" candle socket.

Candle lantern
Tin frame, glass sides, wire guards, factory-made, c. 1860.
Value: $85-$100.

Trammel candle holder
Hand wrought iron, sawtooth, ratchet adjustable to seven heights, c. 1820.
Value: $400-$425.

Wood framed candle lantern
Pine and glass, c. 1840-1850.
Value: $120-$140.

Rush holder
Candle socket counterweight, twisted iron shaft for added strength, c. 1800-1820.
Value: $225-$250.

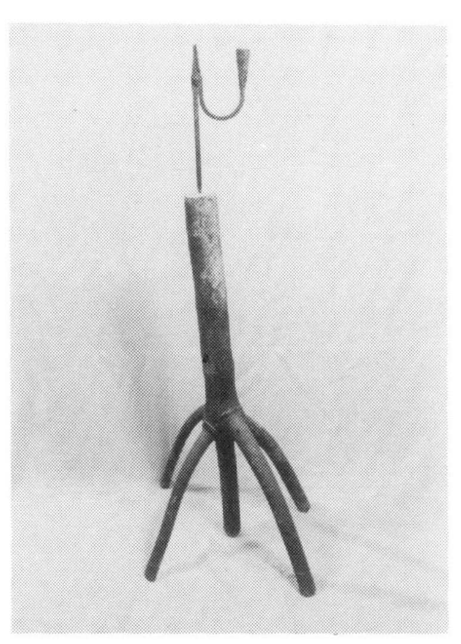

Rush holder
Candle socket counterweight, birch base, New York State, c. 1800-1820.
Value: $325-$350.

Kerosene lamp
Tin, strap handle, tin shade, c. 1860.
Value: $150-$175.

Kerosene came into use in the early 1860s and remained the primary lighting source in the American home until the early 1900s.

Watchman's or lens lantern
Bull's-eye lens to magnify amount of light, whale oil light source, c. 1840.
Value: $95-$110.

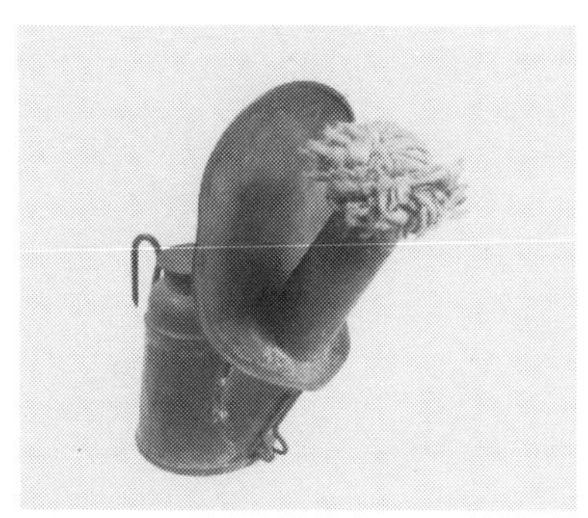

Miner's cap lamp
Coffeepot-shaped font, wick, tin reflector, hinged cover, c. 1900.
Value: $30-$40.

This example and the "Sticking Tommy" candlestick often appear to be much earlier than they are. Both may be found in Sears-Roebuck catalog of the early 1900s.

Kerosene coach lamp
Used in railroad coaches or cars, tin and glass, stamped decoration, c. 1870.
Value: $90-$120.

Railroad lantern
Tin and glass, tin handle, whale oil light source, c. 1850.
Value: $100-$125.

Railway lantern
Wire guard, tin and glass, camphene light source, c. 1850.
Value: $120-$140.

Match holder
Cast iron, designed to be hung on a wall, c. 1870.
Value: $55-$65.

Match holder
C. 1930s, carved by Stanley E. Case.
Value: $85-$95.

Match or spill holder
Brass, c. 1840.
Value: $220-250.

Tin matchbox
C. 1940.
Value: $12-$18.

Kerosene lantern
Brass, burnished, originally nickel-plated, original shade, c. 1880s.
Value: $115-$130.

Kerosene lamp
Nickel-plated over brass, original globe, milk glass shade, c. 1900.
Value: $100-$125.

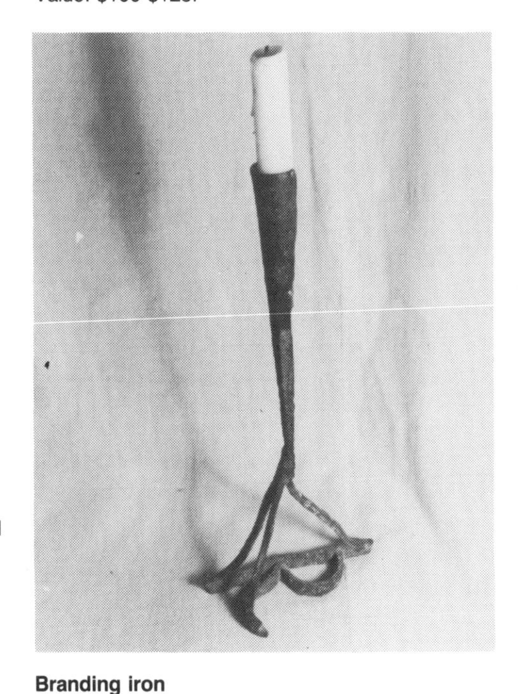

Branding iron
Forged iron, from the American Southwest, c. 1860-1870.
Value: $35-$45.

The wooden handle of this branding iron has been removed and the socket used as a candle holder.

Tin lamps
C. 1900-1920.
Value: $25-$40.

These imported tin lamps are deceiving, because they appear to be very early. They have been imported by the thousands and are relatively inexpensive in most shops.

Coach or carriage light
Glass and brass, polished reflector, c. 1880.
Value: $75-$95.

Dough trough
Cherry, early paint, inset handles, wide dovetails, c. late eighteenth century.
Value: $175-$200.

Decorated tray
Maple, pine bottom, possibly Scandinavian, 14″ diameter, c. 1850.
Value: $135-$165.

Bride's box
"As found" condition, oval, Scandinavian, c. 1850.
Value: $80-$90.

Turned salt bowl
Maple, found in New York State, c. 1860.
Value: $100-$125.

5 Baskets

I bought my first basket, under duress, in 1966. My wife found a rye straw basket with an attached hickory handle and instructed (?) me to pay $35 for it. Thirty-five dollars was a great deal of money to trade for a basket at that time. Baskets had not been "discovered" by the mass of country collectors and many forms that were commonly found then would be considered rare today. In the mid-1960s a cheese basket could be bought for $45.

In thinking back to that period I cannot consciously recall seeing baskets in shops or at antiques shows. This is a relatively common happening. Collectors have a tendency to "see" only certain objects in which they are particularly interested. I have been asked many times if a given item was at a show. After reflection I find that I have no memory of the desired item but someone else may have seen several.

The market for country baskets did not exist a decade ago and most purveyors of antiques did not attempt to sell them. A series of magazine articles that depicted country-oriented homes with baskets hanging from overhead beams was probably a spur to the demand for baskets developing as rapidly as it did. Several books published after 1975 with a myriad of pictures were also a positive influence on basket collectors.

Unlike most other country antiques, baskets are incredibly difficult to date. The materials being used in handcrafted baskets made today are identical to the splints of oak or ash that were used two hundred years ago. Unlike constantly changing furniture styles, basket forms have remained fairly consistent over two centuries.

Exposure to the weather, dirt, and use around the kitchen or garden for a season or two can make a $30 basket purchased at a crafts show into a $120 treasure. There are relatively few individuals producing freshly crafted baskets today. However, as the market and the prices paid for early baskets rise the temptations for prematurely aged baskets to suddenly appear will also increase.

In the spring of 1979 an Ohio dealer offered some excellent half baskets at the Crutcher Indianapolis Antiques Show for $35. This was an obvous bargain until the would-be buyer noticed that the dealer had several more to take the place of those he sold. The same individual once had a floor-to-ceiling stack of pine chopping and dough bowls at another show. He indicated he had purchased them from a collector who had spent twenty years putting the collection together. Apparently the collector also had a weakness for Mexican food because many of the bowls had been patched with lids from tin cans with the names of south of the border communities on them.

Baskets that can be hung from a ceiling tend to be more eagerly sought after than larger, field-type baskets. We see great basket forms that are almost impossible to use in contemporary homes because of their size.

The condition of a basket can dramatically affect its price. Unlike a piece of furniture that can have a series of minor repairs and maintain its value, a basket must be in almost original shape to secure a premium price. The prices of baskets have increased a minimum of 25 percent a year since the mid-1970s. A cheese basket that would be purchased for $110-$125 in 1976 would easily sell for $275-$300 today. Swing-handled baskets have followed cheese baskets as an especially desired form. During the summer of 1977 we purchased two great swing handles for $90 each near Chatham, New York. The same baskets today could not be found for less than $170-$185.

Country baskets were made to be used for storing field crops, draining cheese, collecting eggs, and carrying packages home from the crossroads store. They were inexpensive to buy and were produced by the thousands by traveling basket makers or in small villages or neighborhoods of larger communities that specialized in the making of baskets. They were utilitarian in design and suffered from heavy and frequent use. When a handle was broken or the bottom ripped out, they were usually thrown away or used as kindling rather than being repaired. Baskets and stoneware were similar in the eighteenth and nineteenth centuries in that they were designed to be used. The lengthy household inventories that became part of court records through estate work in the late 1700s and early 1800s seldom if ever list baskets or odd pieces of stoneware.

The basket makers and the potters also shared a premature occupational death. In the late 1890s machine-made baskets and falling prices destroyed the need for more youthful apprentice basket makers and the craft almost disappeared. Potteries also faced the dilemma of refrigeration which took away much of the need for stoneware canning jars, and, eventually, prohibition destroyed the stoneware beer bottle business.

We have no doubt that prices of country baskets will continue to rise. The rise will not be as dramatic as increases in the past decade. There is a price limit somewhere out in space beyond which the desire for a basket grows gradually dim. Most collectors would choose a piece of furniture rather than a basket if the two were comparable in cost. The market is moving in such a fashion that the opportunity to choose between a $300 basket or a $325 country side chair is not far away.

The critical determinant in evaluating a basket is condition. Great basket forms in poor condition have little value. Collectors should not hesitate to pay more for a basket in good repair. Saving a few dollars to purchase a similar basket with several rim breaks or major holes in the sides and bottom is not particularly wise.

Special use forms such as cheese baskets were originally made in a limited supply. Great numbers of cheese baskets are not suddenly going to blossom and appear on the market. Baskets of this type could easily reach $400-$600 in the next several years.

Commercially made market baskets, laundry baskets, and late wicker baskets are not good investments at this point. They are found in such quantity that they hold little interest for most collectors.

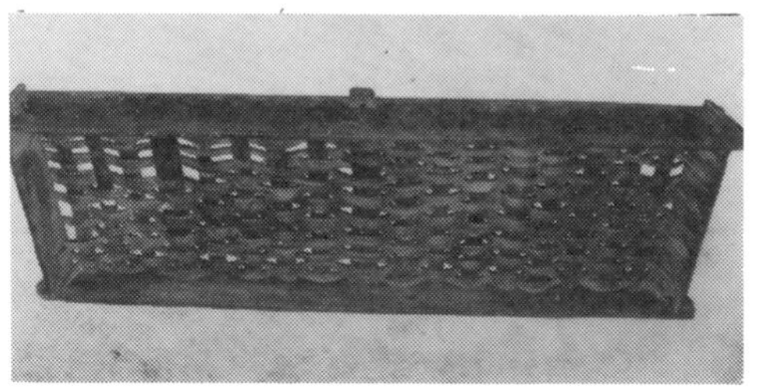

Apple drying basket
Oak splint, pine frame with pin construction, late nineteenth century.
Value: $350-$400.

Orchard basket
Midwestern, hickory splint and handle, mid-nineteenth century, 16″ high x 19″ wide.
Value: $115-$130.

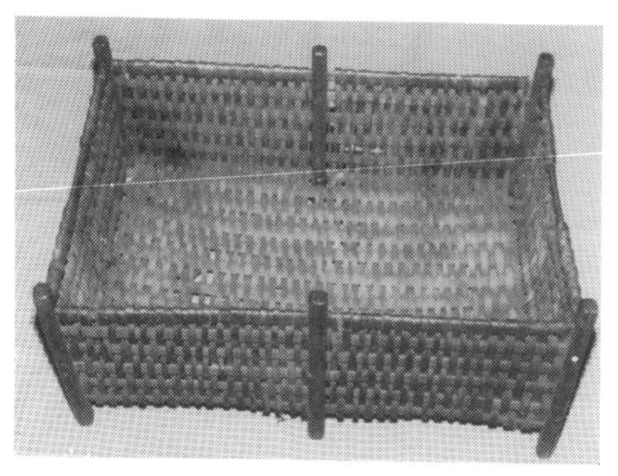

Drying basket
Pegged frame, six legs, inset handles, New England, mid-nineteenth century, rare form.
Value: $400-$475.

Buttocks basket
Possibly made in Tennessee-Kentucky, ash splint, mid-late nineteenth century, 10½″ high to handle x 16″ across.
Value: $95-$115.

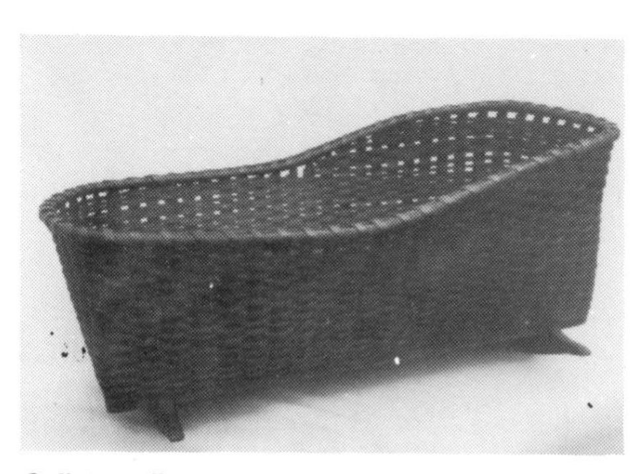

Splint cradle
Solid base, hand-forged nails, traces of red stain, ash splint, oak rims, pine base and rockers, 41″ wide x 16″ high, c. early to mid-nineteenth century.
Value: $650-$800.

Miniature basket
Rib construction, oak splint, found in New England, 5½″ across at widest point, c. mid-nineteenth century.
Value: $145-$165.
Miniature baskets are typically much more valuable than their full-sized counterparts.

Cross-section of utility baskets
Oak and ash splint, late nineteenth century.
Value: $75-$120.

Splint basket
Tennessee, hickory splint, 30″ long x 20″ wide x 12″ high to handle.
Value: $130-$145.

Grocery basket
Oak splint, c. 1930.
Value: $15-$18.

Compare the size of the machine-cut splint in this basket with the other baskets illustrated in this chapter.

Loom basket
Oak splint, painted green, c. late nineteenth century.
Value: $140-$160.

Covered basket
Ash splint, New England, c. mid-nineteenth century.
Value: $120-$135.

Apple picker's basket
Oak splint, maple handle, c. 1890-1910.
Value: $300-$325

Close-up of apple picker's basket
Showing "kicked in" back and hickory loops for belt.

Oak splint baskets
Primarily used for storage, c. late nineteenth century.
Value: $55-$65; $95-$110.

Oak splint workbasket
Single-wrapped rim, demijohn or kicked-in bottom, rib construction, c. mid-1800s.
Value: $100-$115.

This basket form was commonly chosen for baskets designed to hold sewing tools.

Splint workbasket
Carved handles, rib construction, c. mid-1800s.
Value: $75-$95.

Sewing basket
Probably Shaker, New England, splint and rib construction, c. 1880.
Value: $200-$225.

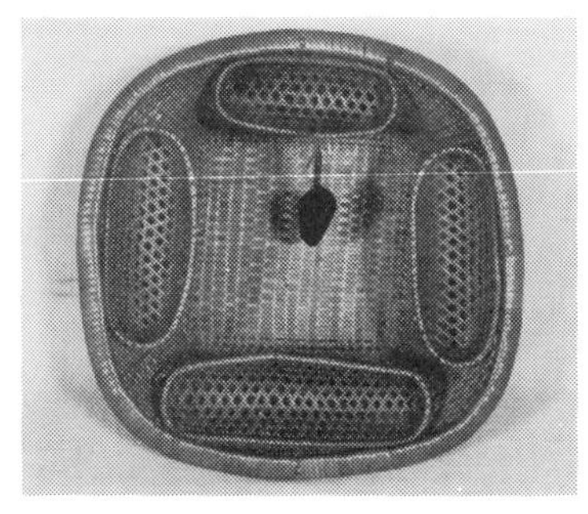

Sewing basket
Shaker, finely woven, heavily wrapped rim, strawberry filled with powdered pumice, c. 1880-1900.
Value: $225-$250.

Sewing baskets and a variety of Victorian bureau and sewing utensils were produced and sold in small shops at the New England Shaker colonies. The Alfred, Maine, Shakers sold many woven poplar sewing baskets and pincushions. The strawberry contains ground pumice that was ideal for sharpening needles.

Bureau box from Alfred, Maine
Shaker, woven poplar, silk lined, front ribbons missing, c. 1880s.
Value: $25-$30.
In mint condition with ribbons —$90-$110.

Shaker trademark
Stamped on bottom of bureau box, c. 1880.

Workbasket
Rib construction, single-wrapped rim, carved handles c. mid-1880s.
Value: $100-$110.

This view of the demijohn bottom provides some indication of the skills of the nineteenth century basket maker who produced this example. A demijohn bottom should add 10 to 20 percent to the value of a basket.

Shaker bureau box
Woven poplar, silk ribbons, and interior lining, c. 1880.
Value: $90-$110

White oak splint storage basket
Called an "oriole" basket in Appalachia, dyed splint, c. 1900.
Value: $115-$125.

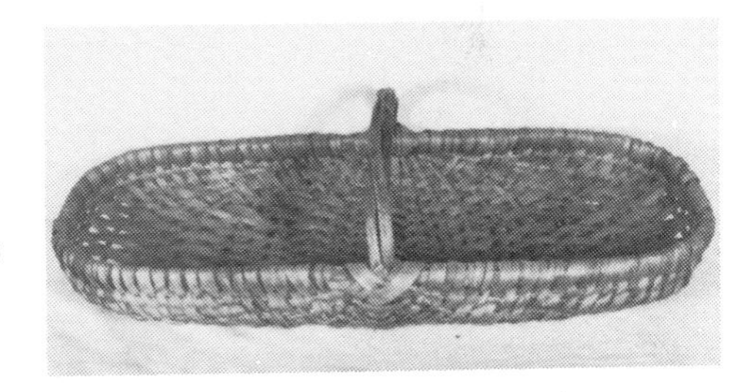

Splint basket for gathering herbs or flowers
Uncommon twisted handle, shallow, New York State, c. 1870.
Value: $210-$225.

Covered buttocks basket
Oak splint, twisted handle, rib construction, nineteenth century.
Value: $300-$375.

The twisted handle provides an extra degree of strength for carrying heavy loads. This is an uncommon basket form.

Willow stick field basket
Crudely constructed, woven willow branches, New York State, c. mid-1800s.
Value: $165-$185.

A willow stick separated from its bark becomes wicker. In the early 1900s, wicker became very popular for use in summer furniture and baskets. This basket has endured more than a century of hard use. Green willow sticks were wrapped around a pine rib frame and allowed to age gracefully while working in the fields and orchards of New York State.

Oblong market basket
Shaker, classic handle shape, initialed "W.B.W.," New England, c. 1850-1860.
Value: $130-$150.

Oblong market basket
Shaker, note the rim wrap, found near Chatham, New York, c. 1850-1860.
Value: $135-$150.

Oblong market basket
Found in New Hampshire, dyed blue splint, splayed sides, c. 1870.
Value: $110-$125.

Compare the form of the Shaker Baskets illustrated with this basket. As the interest in Shaker antiques grows, many items will be mislabeled and sold as Shaker. Shaker baskets and tinware are difficult to identify with any degree of certainty, even by serious collectors.

Rye straw dough basket
Coiled rye straw, banded with hickory or oak splint, probably from Pennsylvania, also called "Mennonite" baskets, c. mid-1800s.
Value: $75-$90.

This bread-raising or dough basket was used in the Mennonite counties of Pennsylvania throughout the 1800s and early 1900s. The top coil was elevated to allow the basket to be hung from a convenient nail. In recent years, rye baskets of questionable age have turned up in many antiques shops. Early baskets should show signs of age, and the splint that binds the rye coils should have developed a patina over time.

Rye basket with hickory handle
Pennsylvania, c. mid 1800s.
Value: $135-$150.

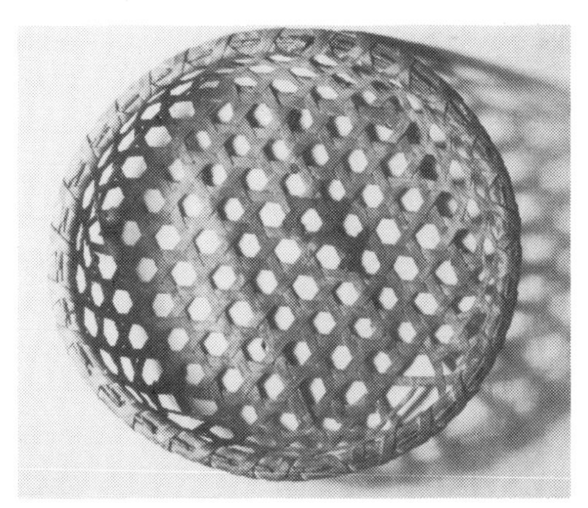

Curd basket
New England, hexagon weave, oak splint, rough condition, c. 1850.
Value: $200-$225

Cheese or curd baskets were used to separate curds and whey. A piece of cheesecloth was spread in the basket, and the basket was placed on a "cheese ladder" over an open crock. The mixture was poured into the basket and the whey filtered into the crock. The curds were bundled in the cloth and allowed to dry slowly.

Cheese ladder
New England, mortised and pegged construction, maple, c. 1850.
Value: $55-$65.

This example was carefully constructed and artfully designed.

Cheese ladder
Found in New York State, crudely constructed, pine, c. 1860.
Value: $30-$35.

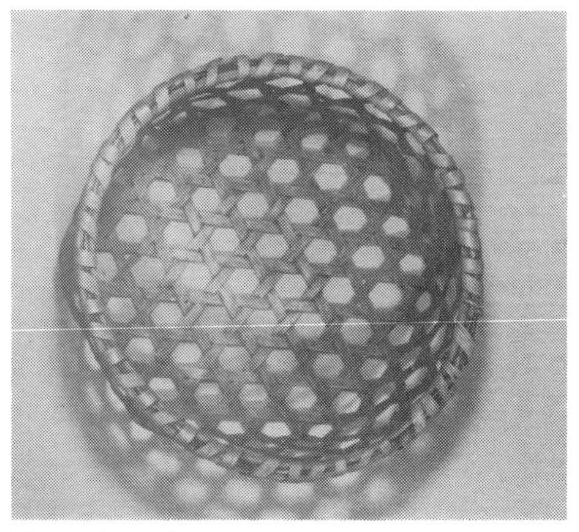

Cheese basket
New England, 19″ diameter, oak splint, c. 1850.
Value: $325-$375.

Cheese basket (bottom)
Shaker, uncommonly well-made, hickory and ash splint, c. 1850.
Value: $400-$450.

In 1977 cheese baskets were priced at about $135-$150. In the summer of 1980 a cheese basket would retail for $300-$350 depending upon its construction and condition.

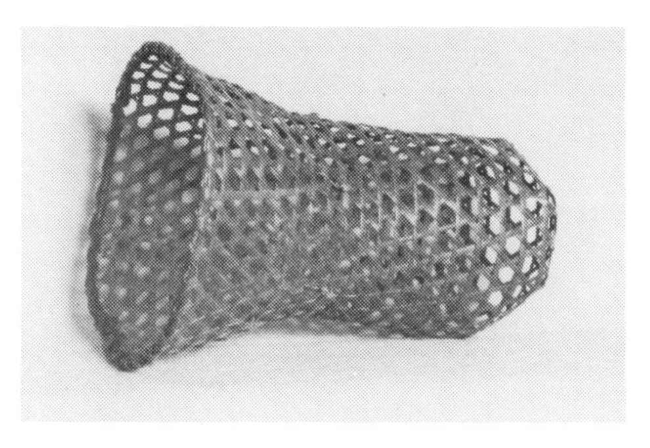

Cheese basket
New England, rare form, hexagon weave, 5″ diameter x 9″ high, c. 1870.
Value: $145-$160.

Windsor cheese strainer
New England, maple and ash with hickory rods, "as found" condition, c. 1820-1830.
Value: $325-$350.

The cheese strainer with attached ladder was used the same as the woven cheese baskets. Windsor or stick construction in this form is rare. The wire repair on the rim does not seriously impair the value of the piece. Early repairs of this type often add to the value of a given piece and make it even more unique.

Splint field or orchard basket
Oak splint, double-wrapped handles, 42″, handle to handle, New England, c. 1860.
Value: $285-$325.

This basket has survived heavy use in excellent condition. It took a master basket maker, using much thickly cut oak splint, a long time to produce this uncommon form.

Large oval field or orchard basket
Single-wrapped rim, inset handles, rib construction, found in Illinois, c. 1860-1880.
Value: $350-$375.

Field baskets characteristically have an open-plaited bottom that allowed any excess dirt or moisture to escape. It also provided an additional opportunity for air to circulate in a filled basket.

Field basket
Carved handles, solid sides, thickly cut splint, open plaited bottom, c. 1850.
Value: $325-$350.

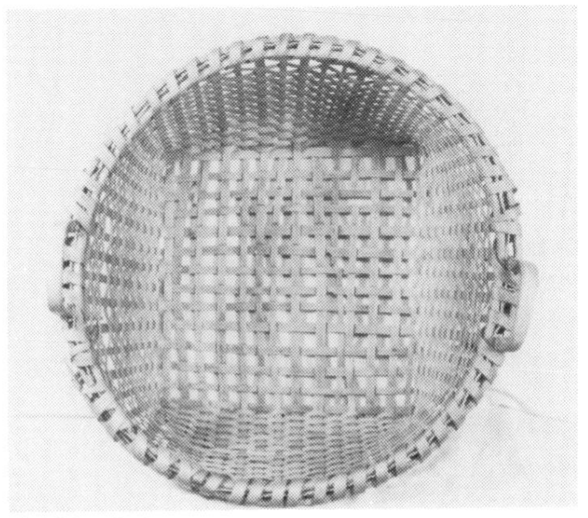

Field basket
Wrapped rim, oak splint, open plaited bottom, carved handles, c. 1860-1880.
Value: $150-$175.

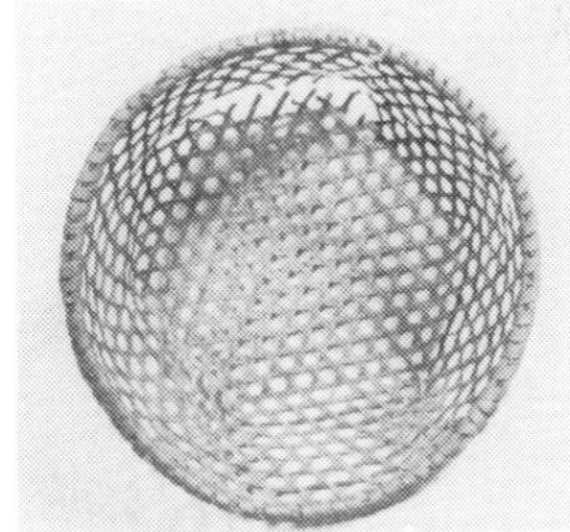

Kitchen food storage basket
New England Shaker, hexagon open weave, damaged side, c. 1850.
Value: $55-$70.

If this basket were in mint condition, it would be worth $200-$250.

If the basket were skillfully repaired it might increase its value to $95-$120. Perhaps, in time, the scarcity of early forms will increase the value of damaged baskets. At this point, great baskets are still being discovered and collectors have not reached the point where they will pay high prices for broken baskets.

Swing-handle basket
Early blue paint, carved bail handle, carved bows, found in Massachusetts, c. 1850.
Value: $275-$325.

Baskets in early paint are rarely found. The value of a basket is increased by 50 to 75 percent if it carries a coat of early blue, red, mustard, or green paint. Baskets in white paint are more commonly found than any other color. Their value is raised 10 to 20 percent over baskets without paint.

The carved bows are fixed to the sides of the basket and allow the handle to swing with a degree of freedom.

Slide-top basket
Ash splint, early forest green paint, possibly Shaker, bulbous sides, 11½" high from handle to basket bottom, c. 1840.
Value: $250-$275.

Baskets of this form were often used for storing feathers. Typically, they are much larger.

Swing-handle basket
Ash splint, carved handle and bows, found in New York State, c. 1850.
Value: $175-$200.

Melon basket
Splint construction over oak ribs, found in Kentucky, a great, worn patina, c. 1860.
Value: $100-$125.

Miniature melon basket
Rib construction, 6″ diameter, found in Ohio, c. 1870.
Value: $115-$125.

Miniature baskets are not as commonly found as the larger forms.

Crudely-made buttocks basket
Oak splint, rib construction, found in Kentucky, c. 1840.
Value: $75-$95.

Buttocks basket
Found in New York State, unusually finely woven oak splint, c. 1860-1870.
Value: $125-$140.

Buttocks basket
Oak rib construction, found in Kentucky, c. 1850-1860.
Value: $95-$110.

Melon basket
Heavy splint handle, rib construction, oak splint, c. 1850-1860.
Value: $85-$95.

Compare this melon basket to the buttocks basket at left. The melon form has a much less pronounced indentation across the bottom than the buttocks basket. Buttocks baskets appear more often in southern Illinois, Kentucky, Tennessee, and West Virginia than in any other section of the country.

Splint basket
Rib construction, double-splint handle, found in Kentucky, c. 1860.
Value: $85-$95.

Splint basket
Rib construction, oak splint, c. 1900-1910.
Value: $60-$75.

Many baskets were constructed during a craft revival in the late 1800s and early 1900s. This basket has the added factor of dyed splint to provide a hint of color.

Hanging storage basket
Crudely-fashioned rib construction, carved handle, c. mid-1800s.
Value: $135-$145.

Storage and drying basket
Carved stick handle, rib construction, four legs, possibly European, c. mid-1800s.
Value: $95-$110.

Hanging basket
Oak splint, rib construction, probably European, c. mid-1800s.
Value: $85-$100.

In recent years, a great influx of western European primitives has disrupted the antiques market. Many collectors have purchased Spanish or English iron or furniture under the mistaken impression they were finding a slice of early America. A firm in southern New York State has gained a national reputation for supplying large quantities of early items from Europe, Spain, and Portugal. Their catalog is an excellent investment and education as to what is currently available. The baskets on this page have the look of imports.

Basket for carrying two pies
Shaker-made, New England, c. 1890-1900.
Value: $130-$150.

Picnic basket
Factory-made, c. 1930.
Value: $35-$45.

Berry basket
Measures 5½″ from top of handle to bottom, oak splint, New Jersey, c. 1850-1860.
Value: $50-$60.

Berry basket
Wooden bottom, 5″ high, iron top and bottom rim, possibly Shaker, c. 1900.
Value: $50-$60.

Cut-plug tobacco tin
Made to resemble wicker basket, c. 1910.
Value: $35-$45.

Clam basket in blue paint
Solid ends, pine frame, hickory double-splint handle, Maine, c. 1900-1920.
Value: $85-$100.

Miniature slide-top basket
Shaker, New England, 5″ from top of handle to bottom, c. 1870.
Value: $110-$125

Slide-top basket
Probably Shaker, ash splint, classic handle form, c. 1900.
Value: $135-$150.

Ash splint field basket
Measures 28″ long x 15″ wide, splint handle, Illinois, c. 1870.
Value: $125-$140.

Field basket
Ash splint, probably Shaker, carved bow handles, 24″

diameter x 20″ high, c. 1870-1880.
Value: $140-$160.

Lift lid basket
Ash splint, carved handles, c. 1870.
Value: $85-$95.

Miniature melon basket
Rib construction, excellent patina, New England, c. 1830-1840.
Value: $95-$115.

Open splint basket
Inset handles, three coats (at least) of early paint, used for storage, c. 1860.
Value: $100-$125.

Field basket
Single-wrapped rim, carved bow handles, open-plaited bottom, oak splint, c. 1850-1870.
Value: $125-$140.

Shaker washhouse basket
Oak splint, carved bow handles, 16″ high x 18″ long x 12″ wide, c. 1850.
Value: $150-$160.

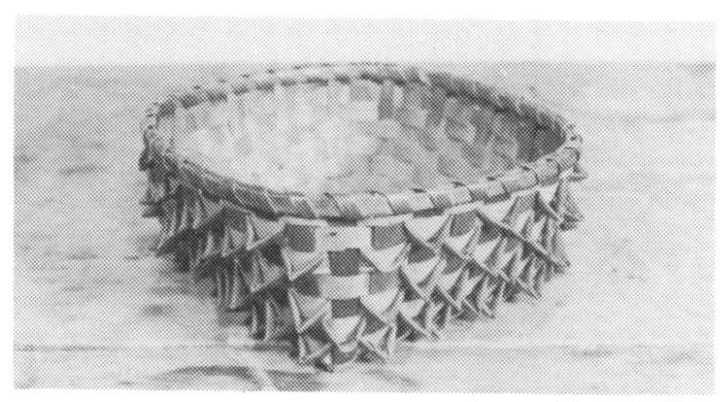

Algonkian Indian "curly" ornamental basket
Found in northwestern New York State, c. early 1900s.
Value: $55-$65.

Many similar baskets were sold at reservation craft booths and in country stores surrounding eastern Indian reservations.

Utility basket
Ash splint, carved bow handles, c. 1860-1870.
Value: $85-$100.

Splint flower basket
Thickly cut oak splint, carved handle, used for gathering small flowers, c. 1880.
Value: $85-$95.

Utility basket
Hickory splint, carved handle, round mouth and square bottom, probably Midwestern, c. 1880.
Value: $85-$95.

Utility basket
Ash splint, carved handle, round mouth and square bottom, probably Midwestern, c. 1880.
Value: $95-$110.

Utility basket
Carved handle, ash splint, Midwestern, c. 1900.
Value: $65-$75.

These baskets were used for light storage in the kitchen or for gathering enough vegetables for a simple meal from the family garden.

The Algonkians used a carefully carved potato dipped into a dye or stain made from a combination of fruits and vegetables to produce a simple design on the splint baskets.

Algonkian basket
Ash splint, 4″ diameter, every other rib painted, dyed splint, c. 1900.
Value: $70-$80.

Covered basket
Algonkian Indian, New England, freehand decoration, c. 1840.
Value: $140-$150.

The quality of workmanship in this basket is superior to the more crudely constructed example at left.

Miniature covered basket
Algonkian Indian, New England, 4½″ x 3½″ x 4″, c. 1840.
Value: $100-$115.

Covered basket
Algonkian Indian, New England, "potato" stamp decoration, c. 1840.
Value: $120-$135.

Covered basket
Algonkian Indian, New England, "potato" stamp decoration, c. 1840.
Value: $145-$175.

The value of the four covered baskets shown is enhanced because they are part of a graduated "put together" nest of six. A "put together" nest of boxes or baskets is a collection of varying backgrounds but similar forms found over the years and displayed together.

Storage basket
Ash splint, double-splint bow handles, diameter of 14″, single-wrapped rim, c. 1870-1880.
Value: $140-$160.

Storage basket
Carved bow handles, red and blue dyed hickory splint, probably Indian made, c. 1870.
Value: $85-$95.

Factory-made wire potato basket
C. 1880-1900.
Value: $50-$60.

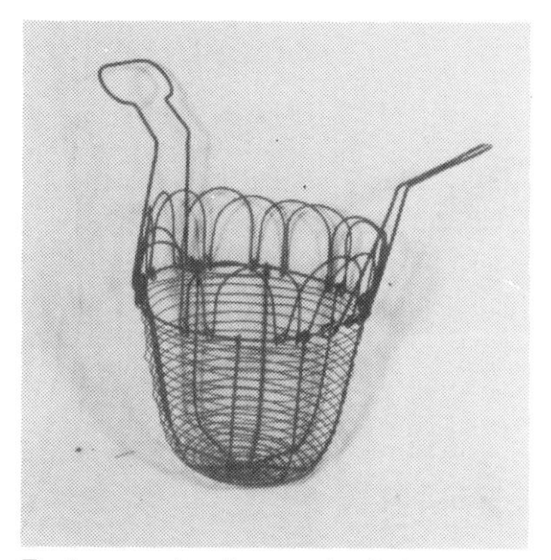

Factory-made wire egg basket
C. 1880-1900.
Value: $35-$45.

Curd or cheese basket
Hexagon weave construction, 26″ diameter, New York State, c. 1850.
Value: $350-$375.

Sweet-grass utility basket
Woven sweet-grass, splint wrapping, Indian made, c. 1850.
Value: $75-$85.

Algonkian open basket
Blade-ash splint, bow handles, dyed decoration, New England, c. 1840.
Value: $75-$90.

Covered basket
Probably Indian-made for the white market, primarily of ash splint, c. 1850.
Value: $120-135.

The Algonkians and Iroquois made these baskets for whites to use as storage containers for hats and clothing.

Fruit basket
Ash splint sides, oak splint plaited bottom, inset handles, splayed sides, c. 1860.
Value: $85-$100.

This early form of the berry basket preceded the mass-produced pine and basswood containers that became popular after 1865.

6 Pottery

For a nineteenth century pottery to be successful it required skilled craftsmen, an ample supply of clay, glazes that would hold up under intense heat, a kiln, roads or a nearby river to transport the pottery and import the clay, and a ready market for the wares.

Potteries and potters were in and out of business often due to fires, explosions, fading markets, and bankruptcies. Seldom did a pottery survive for more than a generation or two of potters. The competition grew to a point that price wars were common and any innovations or new products were quickly duplicated by neighboring potteries.

Most collectors today search diligently for the potter's wares that were carefully decorated with cobalt blue flowers, swirls, birds, or even scenes. The majority of the collectors are primarily collecting design rather than the potter's mark. The uniqueness of the cobalt design is much more tempting to most buyers than the degree of rarity of the mark.

Value in stoneware is determined by the decoration, condition of the piece, and the impressed pottery mark. If all three are found in a single piece the price can be prohibitive for most collectors.

There are many hardcore pottery collectors who search for all the marks of a particular pottery or the products of a particular community that contained several nineteenth century potteries.

In the mid-1960s decorated stoneware with flowers and birds or cobalt swirls would be commonly found for $35-$75 depending on the complexity of the design. Today we seldom see even the most simply brushed bird jugs for less than $150-$175. In 1967 we purchased an unmarked bird jug from a dealer in New York State for $25. The jug later lost its handle when it was run over by a lawn mower.

Prices began a sudden increase in 1970 and continued to rise until about 1975 when an initial peak occurred that lasted several years. After three years of fairly stable prices stoneware began a resurgence in the late 1970s and prices continue to increase today.

The pieces that have increased the most are the more unusual and elaborate in decoration. Mediocre stoneware that was inexpensive in the 1960s is still relatively inexpensive in the 1980s.

Most of the elaborately brush-decorated crocks and jugs were produced after 1850. At approximately that point potteries began to gradually turn away from the ovoid form to pottery with more cylindrical sides. This provided more of an area to decorate than the earlier pieces and potters and their decorators took advantage of it.

A minimal amount of jugs, crocks, and churns with galloping horses, deers and trees, lions, and people were produced in the nineteenth century and few have survived. Prices for great stoneware have risen in the past few years and will continue to do so as more collectors are moved emotionally and financially by American folk art.

For those who do not want to pay $1,900 for a prancing cobalt colt or $3,000 for a brushed scene of nineteenth century seashore bathing beauties more conservative pieces at matching prices may still be found.

Three-gallon ovoid redware jug
Incised "3", swirl of cobalt, ovoid form, New England, c. 1830.
Value: $220-$240.

Ovoid jugs are uncommon and seldom decorated. Incising was a process of scratching a design into the damp surface of a freshly turned piece with a thin slice of sharpened iron.

Two-gallon stoneware jug
No decoration, ovoid form, c. 1830-1840.
Value: $135-$150.

Ovoid jug
Two-gallon, unmarked, brushed cobalt "2", c. 1830-1840.
Value: $135-$150.

Two-gallon stoneware crock
Cobalt blue floral spray, impressed "FB Norton & Co. Worcester, Mass.," c. 1870-1875.
Value: $145-$155.

Compare the later impressed "2" with the early incised "3" on the ovoid jug in photograph at left.

E. and L. P. Norton four-gallon jug
Bennington, Vermont, cobalt floral spray, c. 1861-1881.
Value: $185-$200.

Five-gallon "bird" jug
Gately, Boston, Mass., well-defined "fat" robin, c. 1870.
Value: $250-$275.

Three-gallon "bird" crock
Scatterlee and Mory, Fort Edward, New York, c. 1870.
Value: $225-$250.

Four-gallon "bird" crock
Ottman Bros., Fort Edward, New York, c. 1875.
Value: $275-$325.

Decorated preserve jar
Cowden and Wilcox, Harrisburg, Pa., vine and cobalt grapes, c. 1870-1875.
Value: $210-$225.

Five- and six-gallon decorated jugs appear less often than do the more commonly found one and one-half and three-gallon examples.

In 1862, the Ballard Pottery of Burlington, Vermont, listed four-gallon decorated preserve jars with lids for $9 a dozen. The one and one-half-gallon jars were offered at $5 a dozen.

Batter jug
Unsigned, Albany slip decoration over stoneware, original tin covers, c. 1880.
Value: $95-$110.

In 1899, a Syracuse, New York, pottery was selling similar one and one-half-gallon jugs with tin covers for $4 a dozen.

Decorated stoneware preserve jar
Slip cup bird in cobalt, impressed "C. W. Braun, Buffalo," c. 1865-1870.
Value: $275-$315.

A slip cup was a pottery decorating tool used much like a cake decorator to spread a thin line of cobalt blue slip. Stoneware with slip cup decoration is less commonly found than brush-decorated stoneware. A comparison may be made between the slip cup bird on the Braun jar and the brush decorated bird on the five-gallon jug at right.

Decorated four-gallon "bird" crock
Unsigned, found in New York State, c. 1870-1875.
Value: $230-$275.

Three-gallon "bird" jar
Whites', Utica, originally had a tin lid and bale handle, c. 1875.
Value: $210-$240.

Whites', Utica, three-gallon "bird" jug
Splash of cobalt over impressed signature, c. 1870-1875.
Value: $175-$200.

N. A. White and son two-gallon crock
C. 1850
Value: $165-$175.

Heavily decorated crocks of deep cobalt are uncommon. The cobalt became so expensive that it was necessary for the potteries to water down the slip to make it go farther.

One and one-half-gallon crock from the New York Stoneware Company
Cobalt horsefly decoration, impressed "6", c. 1870.
Value: $150-$175.
(Caraker Collection.)

The impressed "6" probably indicates the size in a series that the pottery made, rather than the number of gallons it held. The horsefly was put on with a slip cup.

Unsigned six-gallon "bird" crock
Combination of brush and slip cup decoration, c. 1860.
Value: $350-$375.

Uncommon four-gallon "duck" crock
W. Hart, Ogdensburgh, rare form for a "bird," c. 1860.
Value: $350-$425.

The standard cobalt bird found on most crocks or jugs appears here. This example took more of a whimsical attitude or a degree of creativity to develop.

Six-gallon crock
Heavily decorated cobalt bird, F. B. Norton, Worcester, Massachusetts, c. 1870.
Value: $350-$400.

After the late-1870s, relatively few heavily decorated pieces of stoneware were created. A network of roads and railways opened up previously captured markets to nationwide distribution of goods. The increased costs of labor and competition forced the potteries to produce stoneware as cheaply as possible and provide decoration only on special order at an increased cost.

Two-gallon jar
Lyons, New York State, heavy cobalt flower, applied ear handles, c. 1860.
Values: $160-$185.

Stoneware jar
J. Norton, Bennington, Vermont, one and one-half-gallon, deep cobalt bird, c. 1859-1861.
Value: $250-$275.

Bennington pottery is relatively easy to date by the impressed signature. J. Norton and Co. operated the pottery between 1859 and 1861. The longest period of ownership was between 1861 and 1881 with the E. and L. P. Norton mark. The value of Bennington stoneware is significantly affected by the impressed mark. The largest period of production and the most common mark is the E. and L. P. Norton.

Bennington two-gallon jug
E. and L. P. Norton, Bennington, Vermont, simple deep blue cobalt flower, c. 1861-1881.
Value: $135-$150

Two-gallon jug
Unmarked, probably Whites', Utica, interesting flower, c. 1870.
Value: $135-$150.

Two-gallon stoneware jar
Brush decoration, blue "2", c. 1850.
Value: $110-$125.

Four-gallon Peoria Pottery crock
Albany slip decoration, molded rather than hand-thrown, c. 1880-1890.
Value: $85-$95.

Peoria Pottery is considerably more valuable in Peoria County, Illinois, than in any other area of the nation. Many other late examples from local potteries are eagerly sought in a limited geographic area, and hardly recognized in the rest of the country. Peoria pottery is interesting because Christopher Fenton of Bennington, Vermont, and the legendary pottery there helped to establish the Illinois pottery.

Butter crocks in original condition are difficult to find with an original lid. A collector should check the lid to make sure it has not been a recent addition. The glazes, decoration, and wear on the crock and lid should match.

Stoneware crock
Stenciled decoration, two-gallon, Hamilton and Jones, Greensboro, Pennsylvania, c. 1875.
Value: $110-$120.

Butter crock
Applied ear handles, cobalt decoration, original lid, brushwork decoration, c. 1860.
Value: $225-$250.

Late two-gallon Midwestern jug
Buff color, cylindrical sides, no decoration, c. 1900.
Value: $18-$22.

Compare the jugs on page 119 with this jug. Note how the ovoid or pear shape has been transformed over about 75 years to a cylindrical form. It is possible to judge the relative age of a piece of stoneware by the degree to which the piece is caught between the ovoid and cylindrical form. It was a gradual change and much can be learned by careful study.

One-gallon jug
Deep cobalt decoration, c. 1875-1880.
Value: $75-$85.

Two-gallon jug
Impressed, "2", cobalt flower, c. 1870-1875.
Value: $80-$85.

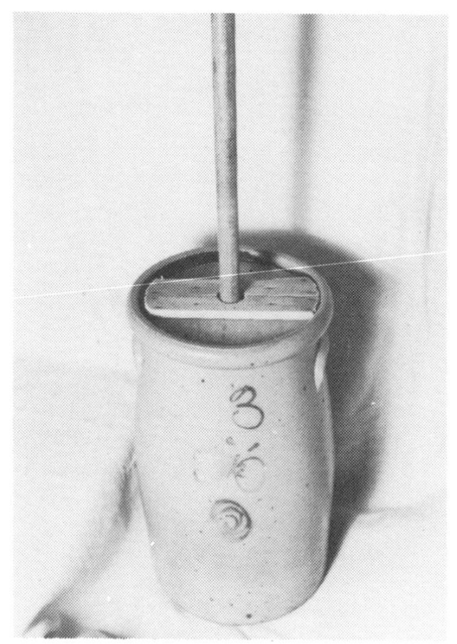

Three-gallon stoneware churn
Midwest, late swirl decoration, c. 1880-1890.
Value: $110-$120.

The wooden dasher and lid are original to the churn. Churns of this type were made well into the 1900s. The swirl decoration and hastily drawn "3" are indicative of the dying days of decorative stoneware.

Stoneware churn
Albany slip, probably Midwestern, c. 1880, unmarked.
Value: $85-$95.

Stoneware churn
Deep cobalt brushed flower and leaf, three-gallon, probably New York State, unmarked, c. 1850.
Value: $160-$185.

Molded stoneware bottle
Splash of cobalt on the neck, marked "Green and Clark," c. 1880.
Value: $50-$55.

Stoneware spitton
Unsigned, brushwork decoration, c. 1850.
Value: $200-$225.

Spittoons were in the precarious position of being constantly underfoot. They were stepped on, kicked, and periodically cleaned. It is not surprising that few have survived.

Stoneware jar
Applied ear handles, unsigned, probably made in New York State, c. 1860-1870.
Value: $115-$125.

Many pieces of stoneware carry a cobalt decoration that is difficult to specifically identify. This particular example could be a variety of things. If it were a side view of a man with his arm cocked in a throwing position it would certainly be rare.

Butter crock
Stoneware, sold by the thousands at turn of century, molded rather than thrown, rarely found with lid and handle.
Value: $65-$75.

Stenciled jug
Hamilton and Jones, Greensboro, Pennsylvania, c. 1865-1870.
Value: $85-$95.

Stenciling initially became popular in the early 1850s when the competition between potteries forced a quicker means of decorating stoneware. Some magnificent examples of Hamilton and Jones stoneware are occasionally found that combine stenciling with elaborate brush work.

Stoneware jar
Stenciled decorated, two-gallon, Hamilton and Jones, Greensboro, Pennsylvania, c. 1875.
Value: $140-$160.

Stoneware preserve jar
Unmarked, probably Midwestern, c. 1875-1880.
Value: $50-$60.

Redware pitcher
Found in southern Illinois, unmarked, c. 1830-1840.
Value: $75-$90.

Cream pitcher
Albany slip, unmarked, c. 1870s.
Value: $45-$55.

Pitcher
Sponge decorated, unmarked, c. 1875-1885.
Value: $115-$140.

Pitcher
Sponge decorated, unmarked, c. 1875-1885.
Value: $135-$145.

Pitcher
Unmarked, probably Midwestern, stoneware, c. 1880.
Value: $45-$55.

Pitcher
Brush decorated, probably Pennsylvania, unmarked, c. 1850s.
Value: $225-$250.

Decorated pitchers are extremely difficult to find. Prices on butter crocks, pitchers, and spittoons have soared in recent years because of their scarcity. Rarely are marked (signed) examples discovered.

Redware jar
Unmarked, found in Pennsylvania, c. 1840.
Value: $65-$75.

The first pottery produced in America was made from the red clay that was available in vast quantities along the Eastern seaboard. The redware pottery was fired at relatively low temperatures that produced a brittle product. Because of its inability to be watertight, it was necessary to seal or glaze the redware.

Redware jar
Unmarked, c. 1830.
Value: $85-$95.

A redware pie plate or serving plate that has its surface decorated with a word or phrase written in slip is worth three to five times a conventional undecorated plate. Pie plates were glazed and decorated only on the inside surface. The pie was removed from the plate in which it was baked before it was cut and served.

Redware pie plate
Diameter, 8″, heavily carboned bottom, found in Ohio, glazed interior, c. 1820.
Value: $80-$90.

Redware apple butter pot
Unmarked, glazed interior, found in Pennsylvania, c. 1840.
Value: $135-$145.

The only decoration on this pot is the incised lines on the shoulder or upper portion. This pot was used to serve apple butter at the dinner table. Pots used for storage were made without handles.

Redware milk pan
Diameter, 10″, found in Pennsylvania, unmarked, c. 1840.
Value: $120-$130.

Redware pots
Incised lines, found in Pennsylvania, unmarked, glazed interiors, c. 1840.
Value: $75-$85.

Apple butter pot
Green glaze, found in Ohio, unmarked, for table use, c. 1830-1840.
Value: $140-$175.

A potter had a variety of glaze colorings from which to choose, including black, red, orange, brown and yellow. The green glaze was made from oxidized copper that was expensive and often difficult to obtain.

Stoneware jug
Unmarked, one-gallon size, Albany slip covered, probably Midwestern, c. 1900.
Value: $30-$35.

This jug was found while digging a well on the Dale Troyer farm near Hudson, Illinois. It is not uncommon to find pottery shards or fragments, but seldom is an intact piece discovered.

Redware preserve jar
Deep brown glaze, found in Ohio, unmarked, c. 1840-1850.
Value: $70-$85.

Stoneware jar
Molded rather than hand-thrown, Albany slip covered, c. 1900.
Value: $15-$25.

Yellowware was a popular item in the mail order catalogs of the late 1800s and early 1900s. The pottery was molded rather than hand thrown and available in sets of varying size.

Yellowware is found with decorative brands of blue, white, black, or brown.

Stoneware canning jar
Two-gallon size, stenciled decoration, c. 1880.
Value: $65-$75.

Yellowware mixing bowl
Diameter, 9″, molded, unmarked, c. 1900.
Value: $30-$35.

Yellowware mixing bowl
Diameter, 8″, molded, c. 1900.
Value: $30-$35.

Stoneware inkwell
Glazed, unsigned, pierced for three quill pens, recessed dipping well, c. 1840.
Value: $75-$85.

Stoneware cream pitcher
Held less than a pint, 5″ high, unsigned, dark exterior glaze, c. 1870.
Value: $55-$65.

Stoneware jar
Incised lines, unsigned, c. 1880.
Value: $50-$55.

Redware pie plates
Unsigned, coggled edges, unglazed bottoms, 8″ diameter.
Value: $80-$90.

Fifteen Pieces of Pottery Advertised in 1973

When we began this project we decided it was equally as important to have an understanding of prices in the recent past as it is to be aware of the current market trends. In the early 1970s, stoneware escalated dramatically in value at auctions and antiques shows. We have gathered the descriptions and asking prices of fifteen unusual pieces of decorated stoneware that were advertised in 1973.

Two-gallon Whites' Utica "bird" crock — fan tail bird perched on branches — $85.

Three-gallon crock, Warner, West Troy, N.Y., large flying eagle with banners in its beak — $325.

One-gallon jug, signed "Boston," decorated with a brushed large codfish, $500.

Four-gallon crock, Ottman Bros., Ft. Edward, N.Y., large basket filled with fruit in cobalt, $300.

Two-gallon jug, large urn-shaped vase with a bouquet of flowers, missing handle, $300.

One-and-one-half-gallon crock, detailed bird on a branch, Underwood, Ft. Edward, $65.

Two-gallon crock, incised bird on front and back, ears have broken off, $1,000.

Preserve jar, Bell, Cornwall, N.Y., impressed "1" with impressed leaves around it, $50.

Flask, 8″ tall, unmarked, $35.

Three-gallon crock, human hand forming the "O.K." sign, West Troy, N.Y., $385.

Four-gallon crock, large five-pointed star, "4" on reverse side, $300.

Two-gallon jug, E. and L. P. Norton, highly stylized flower, $65.

Two-gallon jug, Smith and Day, Norwalk, Connecticut, ovoid-brush decoration across name, $65.

Three-gallon churn, Whites' Utica, four 1″ brushed bands, $100.

Two-gallon crock, semi-ovoid, "Pottery Works," two brushed leaves, $90.

Selected 1977 Stoneware Prices from Garth's Auction

Stoneware jug, blue transfer label, "Casey Bros., Scranton, PA." and "Pasteur Chamberland Filter Co., Dayton, Ohio," 7½", $27.50.

Stoneware bottle, "Vimo, Ginger Beer, Cleveland, Ohio," 6½" high, $11.

Stoneware flask, 8" high, $37.50.

Six-gallon stoneware double-handled jar, signature in cobalt, "Lampert, Wenport," 19" high, $37.50.

Stoneware jar, simple leaf in cobalt, 10¼" high, $27.50.

Four-gallon butter crock, impressed signature, "A. O. Whittemore, Havana, N.Y.," well-drawn bird in cobalt, $200.

Two-gallon jug, "J. and E. Norton, Bennington, Vt.," swirled design in cobalt, $135.

Two-gallon ovoid jug, "I. M. Mead," brushed cobalt flower, $105.

Three-gallon stoneware jug, "3" in cobalt, 14½" high, $17.50.

Miniature stoneware advertising jug, incised label, "Husch Bros., Louisville, Ky.," 3" high, $14.

Four-gallon stoneware jar, stenciled label, "William and Reppert, Greensboro, Pa.," 14" high, $27.50.

Six-gallon stoneware jug, cobalt label, "Grant and Colfax 1868," 16½" high, $95.

Stoneware jar, stenciled cobalt label, "T. F. Reppert, Greensboro, Pa.," 9¾" high, $32.50.

Stoneware jar, stenciled label, "Hamilton and Jones, Greensboro, Pa.," 8" high, $45.

Redware plate, four-line yellow slip decoration with green, coggled edge, mint, 11½" diameter, $375.

Redware pitcher, greenish tan glaze, 7¾" high, $15.

Redware plate, yellow slip design with splashes of green and a clear shiny glaze, 8" diameter, $100.

Stoneware batter pitcher, Albany slip, exterior has worn painted flower, 7¾" high, $2.

Stoneware jug, impressed signature, "N.Y. Stoneware Company," simple cobalt leaf design, 14" high, $37.50.

Two-gallon stoneware batter pitcher, "E. Bishop, near Burlington, Ohio," blue brushed design at spout, 13½", $75.

Three-gallon jar, "E. A. Montell, Olean, N.Y.," brushed cobalt flower, 10¾" high, $65.

Three-gallon stoneware jar, "T. Reed," brushed cobalt tulip, 11½" high, $195.

Stoneware canning jar, cobalt blue brushed designs, 9½" high, $70.

Two-gallon batter pitcher, flower and squiggly lines with "1843" in cobalt slip, 13¾" high, $280.

Ten-gallon stoneware crock, comic drawing of old woman with curly hair in cobalt slip, 13½" diameter x 17¼" high, $595.

Six-gallon stoneware crock, incised cow, blue cobalt, "Gardiner Stone Ware, Manufactory, Gardiner, Me.," $55.

Three-gallon stoneware ovoid jug, cobalt blue brushed on at handle, 16¾" high, $45.

Stoneware batter pitcher, brush floral design in cobalt blue, $300.

Bennington covered jar, "1849" mark, $265.

Stoneware "bird" crock, "New York Stoneware Co., North Edward, N.Y., 6," modern wooden lid, 8" high, $105.

Five-gallon crock, three incised eagles, each with spear and banner, 12" high, $85.

Stoneware butter crock, brushed blue feather designs, 8½" diameter, $165.

Three-gallon crock, hen pecking corn in cobalt, 10½" high, $165.

Small wooden washboard, redware insert in wooden frame, 7" x 13½", $37.50.

Stoneware jar, applied handles, brushed blue floral band, 13½" high, $95.

Five-gallon stoneware jug, "Weading and Belding, Brantford, Ohio," brushed flower, 18½" high, $65.

Three-gallon stoneware crock, gilt-work decoration, 13½" high, $75.

Auction Prices of Pottery July, 1977

Some excellent insights into the stoneware market can be made by studying the results of an auction in Duncansville, Pennsylvania, in July, 1977.

The following items were especially noteworthy among the more than four-hundred pieces of stoneware sold at the third annual auction:

John Burger, Rochester, six-gallon crock, large elk with two trees in deep cobalt, with two large cracks, $950.

Six-gallon jar, brushed cobalt decoration of blue morning glories above two women and a small child, all within an open wreath, $1,350.

A. O. Whittemore, four-gallon crock, Havana, New York, small cobalt house with five windows and two chimneys surrounded by weeds, $550.

West Troy, New York, five-gallon crock, large dog in cobalt in front of a fence, $800.

S. Skinner and Co., Picton, C. W., three-gallon jar, cobalt bird with fish in its mouth, $550.

Two-gallon jug, Ottman Bros. and Co., Fort Edward, New York, cobalt long nosed man seated on a keg drinking from a bottle under "CENTENNIAL," $925.

Hamilton and Jones, Greensboro, Pa., four-gallon jar, heavily stenciled, 14¼″ high, $75.

Ovoid jug, crudely drawn running rabbit, 14″ high, $275.

"M. A. Ingalls, Liquor Dealer, Little Falls," two-strap handles, five-gallons, $50.

Three-gallon crock, chicken pecking corn in cobalt blue, 10½″ high, $230.

Cowden and Wilcox, "Man in the Moon," jar, $500.

One-gallon "bird" decorated batter jar, minus tin spout caps and bale handle, repaired ear, $120.

Forty-Eight Pieces of Stoneware Advertised in 1980

Jugs

One-gallon, 10″ tall, "Wm. Radams Microbe Killer Co.," $30.

One-gallon, 10½″ tall, c. 1900, unsigned, molded, brown and white, $12.

Three-gallon, 16″ tall, E. Norton, cobalt flower, $130.

One-gallon, 11″ tall, signed "Haxstun Ottman," cobalt bird, $165.

One-gallon, 12″ tall, Geddes, New York, cobalt decoration, of "K. P. and Co.," $65.

One-gallon, 11½″ tall, N. White and Co., cobalt flying dove, $335.

Two-gallon, 14″ tall, ovoid, c. 1820, unsigned, incised standing bird, $1,500.

Two-gallon, 15″ tall, unsigned, ovoid, brushed tulip, base chip, $150.

Three-gallon, 16″ tall, Jacob Caire, incised bird 8″ long with detail, $1,100.

Two-gallon 13¼″ tall, W. A. Lewis, 6″ long cobalt bird, $300.

Three-gallon, 14½″ tall, C. Hart, cobalt flower and stem, $115.

One-gallon, 11″ tall, J. Norton, cobalt bird, $325.

One-gallon, chicken pecking corn in deep cobalt, Ballard and Scott, Cambridgeport, Massachusetts, $395.

Three-gallon, 15½″ tall, West Troy, New York, large blue bird, $170.

Two-gallon, 14½″ tall, Roberts, Binghamton, New York, great bird covering most of the front of the jug, $295.

Two-gallon, ovoid, J and C Hart, Sherburne, New York, cobalt "2", $135.

One-gallon, 11½″ tall, Whites' Utica, swirl "pine tree" in deep cobalt, $75.

One-gallon, 11″ tall, Haxstun and Company, Fort Edward, New York, simple cobalt flower, $65.

One-half-gallon, 9″ tall, c. 1900, unsigned, no decoration, cream-colored body, $9.

Two-gallon, 14¼″ tall, Whites' Utica, "flamingo," in deep cobalt looking over its shoulder, $225.

Crocks

One-and-one-half-gallon, 8½″ tall, fern in cobalt blue, $70.

Two-gallon, 9½″ tall, unsigned, cobalt bird on a branch, $160.

Six-gallon, 13″ tall, N. A. White and Son, Utica, New York, large deep cobalt orchid, $225.

Four-gallon, 12″ tall, West Troy, New York, simple bird on a branch, $175.

Three-gallon, 10″ tall, unsigned, rim chips, deep cobalt bird, $160.

Four-gallon, 11″ tall, E. Norton and Co., large cobalt flower, $135.

One-and-one-half gallon, 8½″ tall, Brady and Ryan, blue bird on a branch, $150.

Three-gallon, 10″ tall, unsigned, cobalt sketch of a man in uniform, profile, $550.

Two-gallon, 9½″ tall, Burger and Lang, deep cobalt flower, $165.

Three-gallon, 10½″ tall, New York Stoneware Co., great spread winged bird in deep cobalt, landing on a stump, $800.

Two-gallon, 9½″ tall, unsigned, fat bird on a branch, $185.

Two-gallon, 9½″ tall, S. Hart, two birds on a branch, $185.

Three-gallon, crock, 10½″ tall, Brady and Ryan, Ellenville, New York, chicken pecking corn in cobalt, $255.

Two-gallon, 9″ tall, unsigned, deep cobalt bird on a log, $175.

Two-gallon, 8½″ tall, J. Burger, Rochester, New York, two feathers with a cobalt swirl inside, $145.

Two-gallon, 9½″ tall, Haxstun and Company, Ft. Edward, New York, fat bird on a branch, $175.

Pitchers

Six-quart, 11″ tall, unsigned, cobalt bird, repaired crack, $250.

One-gallon, 10″ tall, unsigned, simple cobalt bird on a branch, $775.

One-gallon, 11″ tall, signed J. Burger, geometric cobalt design and "1", $335.

One-and-one-half gallon, pitcher, West Troy, New York, large cobalt feather, $395.

One-gallon, 11½″ tall, Lyons, New York, deep cobalt bird on a branch, $775.

Miscellaneous stoneware

"I.O.O.F. No. 15," lodge hall spittoon, unsigned, 5½″ diameter, $185.

Two-gallon covered jar, 11″ tall, W. H. Farrar/Geddes, New York, deep cobalt flowers and stems, ovoid, $245.

Batter pail, one-gallon, 9¼″ tall, unsigned, no lid, $33.

Churn, three-gallon, 14″ tall, E. S. Fox, Athens, New York, ovoid, double cobalt flower, $295.

One-gallon, ovoid jar, 11″ tall, Warner, West Troy, New York, cobalt swirl, $100.

Butter crock, 7¼″ tall, unsigned, original lid, cobalt flowers and vines, three- to four-gallon size, $395.

7 Shaker Antiques

Ann Lee, the founder and spiritual leader of the Shaker movement, was born in Manchester, England, in 1756. She was one of eight children raised by a struggling blacksmith in the midst of the Manchester slums. Lee married Abraham Standerin and had four children, all of whom died at birth or in early infancy.

After a series of religious revelations and brief periods of imprisonment for her religious beliefs, Lee and a small group of followers immigrated to what is now New York State in 1774. In 1776 Lee and some fellow Shakers established the first permanent colony in Niskeyuna. Lee traveled throughout New York, Massachusetts, and Connecticut gathering converts for several years prior to her death in 1784.

We have included a series of brief questions and answers that, hopefully, will provide some insights into the Shaker movement and collecting Shaker artifacts today.

What were the largest Shaker colonies?

Union Village, Ohio: 600 in 1823.

Pleasant Hill, Ky.: 500 in 1830.

New (Mt.) Lebanon, N.Y.: 600 in the 1850s.

By 1862 Union Village had only 100 members and Pleasant Hill had 250 members.

What was the total number of Shaker members during its two centuries of existence in the United States?

Approximately 16,000 to 17,000 members in nineteen colonies were actively involved with the Shakers from 1774 to date.

What was the official name for the Shaker movement?

United Society of Believers in Christ's Second Appearing (Coming).

Where were the Shaker colonies or branches that were in operation for only a brief time?

Small groups were started in Georgia, New York, Indiana, Ohio, Massachusetts, Florida, and Maine. In the listings of the Shaker colonies that frequently appear, these colonies seldom are included, with the possible exception of West Union (Busro), Indiana.

What restrictions were placed on a Shaker's day-to-day life?

Periodically a list of what was and was not acceptable was issued to the membership. The Millennial Laws were passed by word of mouth initially and eventually by printed documents. The Laws covered almost every aspect of a member's existence. We have selected a few to illustrate the extent of the regimentation. The brothers and sisters could *not* do the following:

a. Shake hands with a "world's" woman without confessing it.
b. Employ a "world's" doctor.
c. Pick fruit on the Sabbath.
d. Have watches and umbrellas.
e. Have any money privately.

Which factors brought about the decline of the Shaker movement?

a. The first and second generations of Shaker leaders were replaced by less skillful leaders who could not maintain the industries and recruit new members.
b. The rise of the factories in the industrial North after the Civil War made mass-produced household goods more available and forced the Shakers to close down many of their areas of handcrafted production.
c. The nation's changing philosophy toward material goods and increased amounts of leisure time brought about internal changes within the Shaker way of life.
d. The Shakers could no longer hold their younger believers and found it increasingly more difficult to recruit new members.
e. As the nineteenth century wore on and the growing disparity in the ratio of Shaker men to Shaker women increased, the number of skilled craftsmen diminished significantly.
f. The increased wealth of the Shakers brought on by rising land values was coupled with a falling membership that forced the Shakers to hire outside workers or sell their holdings.

How do collectors determine what colony produced a particular piece?

It is extremely difficult to precisely determine where or when a Shaker box, basket, or case piece was produced. Due to declining numbers, relatively few pieces of furniture were made after 1870. The Shakers did continue to produce chairs for the "world" at Mount Lebanon until almost the mid-point of the twentieth century. The furniture is also difficult to date or place geographically because few pieces were signed or dated. It is important to remember that the only pieces of furniture that were made for the world were a variety of chairs and footstools, and that at the peak of membership in the early 1850s there were only 6,000 Shaker members. Thus, the limited production of Shaker furniture and the fact that growing numbers of individuals, restorations, and museums have been building collections since the late 1920s does not leave many examples left to be discovered.

Which Shaker antiques are the easiest for today's collectors to find?

The numbered (0-7) production rocking chairs are probably the most plentiful remnants of the Shakers' work. The more common are the middle sizes (3-4). The child's sizes (#0 and #1) are less commonly found.

The woven poplar "fancy" boxes that were produced for sale to tourists and visitors at several of the eastern colonies also usually are available. The "fancy" poplar bureau and sewing boxes were made and sold well into the twentieth century.

Chronological List of Shaker Communities

Watervliet, New York	1787-1938
Mount Lebanon, New York	1787-1947
Hancock, Mass.	1790-1960
Harvard, Mass.	1791-1919
Enfield, Conn.	1792-1917
Tyringham, Mass.	1792-1875
Alfred, Maine	1793-1931
Canterbury, N.H.	1793 - still in operation
Enfield, N.H.	1793-1918
Sabbathday Lake, Maine	1793 - still in operation
Shirley, Mass.	1793-1908
West Union, Indiana	1810-1827
South Union, Ky.	1811-1922
Union Village, Ohio	1812-1910
Watervliet, Ohio	1813-1900
Pleasant Hill, Ky.	1814-1910
Whitewater, Ohio	1824-1907
Groveland, N.Y.	1826-1892
North Union, Ohio	1826-1889

Shaker Chronology

1736	Ann Lee born
1758	Ann Lee becomes a "Shaking Quaker"
1762	Lee marries Abraham Standerin
1762-1766	Four children born to the Standerins and die shortly after birth. Lee is jailed for breaking the Sabbath. While imprisoned for a brief period Ann has revelations that lead her to adopt the title of "Mother" Ann
1774	Eight "Shaking Quakers" come to New York on the *Mariah*
1783	Mother Ann dies in Watervliet, New York
1783-1826	Nineteen Shaker communities in eight states are opened from Maine to Kentucky

1868	Shaker chair industry begins on a large scale
1890	Mount Lebanon obtains a telephone system
1961	Last male Shaker, Brother Delmer Wilson, dies
1980	Surviving Shaker communities at Canterbury and Sabbathday Lake

Sabbathday Lake, Maine, Auction

June 20, 1972

Shaker antiques have been collected by a growing number of individuals since the publication in the late 1920s of an article by Edward and Faith Andrewson in the magazine *Antiques*. To understand prices today it might be worthwhile to look back at a major Shaker auction in 1972 and another Maine auction held in late 1979.

Dasher butter churn, 20″ tall, piggin handle, $500.
Watervliet, twin size bed, maple, wooden rollers, $475.
Flour bag, "Shaker mills," New Glouster, $230.
One "hank" of Shaker-made thread in blue, $27.50.
Catalog of "fancy" goods, $100.
Handled laundry basket, signed Sarah Collins, 14″ x 19″ x 8″ deep, $40.
Large spinning wheel, $375.
Seedbox with Mt. Lebanon label, $162.50.
Hancock small swift in yellow paint, $175.
Bottle, 9″, aqua, label reading "Shaker Pickles," $162.
Alfred sewing desk, 12 drawers and pull-out slide, butternut and maple, $3,250.

Portland, Maine, Shaker Auction

October 23, 1979

Full-sized, signed spinning wheel, $450.
One-drawer stand, turned legs, mushroom pull on drawer, yellow paint under varnish, $500.
Two-piece cast iron stove with penny feet and wrought iron shovel, $1,000.
Bentwood rocker in natural finish, $475.
Early herb drying rack, 74″ x 28″, $800.
Slat-back rocking chair, red paint, homemade shawl or cushion rail, $170.
Two wire rug whips with wooden handles, $65 each.
Cherry 24″ ruler (damaged), $50.
Oval fingered box, natural finish, with cover, $180.
Dusting brush, 14″, maple handle, $70.
Miniature sieve, 4″, $65.
Refinished knife and fork box, $80.
Pedestal pincushion, 6″, with thread holder, $80.
Flour bag, "Shaker Mills, New Glouster," has a picture of a flour mill on it, $190.
Flour bag with a train, $225.
Mount Lebanon side chair, with tilters, natural finish, $800.

Mount Lebanon was known as New Lebanon prior to 1861. These boxes were distributed to the seed dealers to display on their counters.

Shaker combs
C. late nineteenth century.
Value: $60-$70 (pair).

Tin strainer
Attributed to the Harvard, Massachusetts, Shakers, c. 1860.
Value: $50-$60.

Tin cheese or curd drainer
C. 1870.
Value: $160-$175.

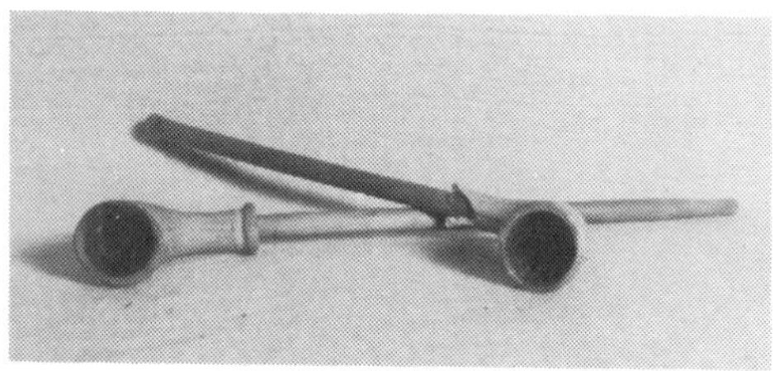

Clay pipes
Attributed to the Mount Lebanon Shakers, c. 1870.
Value: $25-$35.

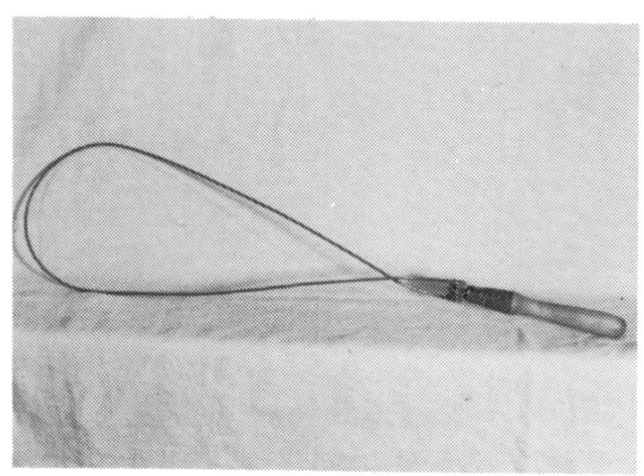

Rug beater
Wire with maple handle, "Levi Shaw, Mt. Lebanon, N.Y.," c. 1880.
Value: $110-$125.
(J.A. Honegger collection)

Tin lamp filler can
Used to fill kerosene lamps, c. 1870-1880.
Value: $90-$110.

Dustpan and whisk broom
Broom made from broom corn, turned maple handle, c. 1850.
Value: Broom - $60-$70.
Dustpan - $110-$120.

Spice chest
New England, six drawers, pine and maple, red stain, c. 1850.
Value: $275-$300.

Yarn swift
Harvard, Massachusetts, maple, yellow wash or stain, c. 1880.
Value: $200-$225.

Clothes hanger, dusting brush
Turned maple handle, type sold in Shaker community shops, c. 1890-1900.
Value: Dusting brush - $95-$110.
Maple hanger - $50-$55.

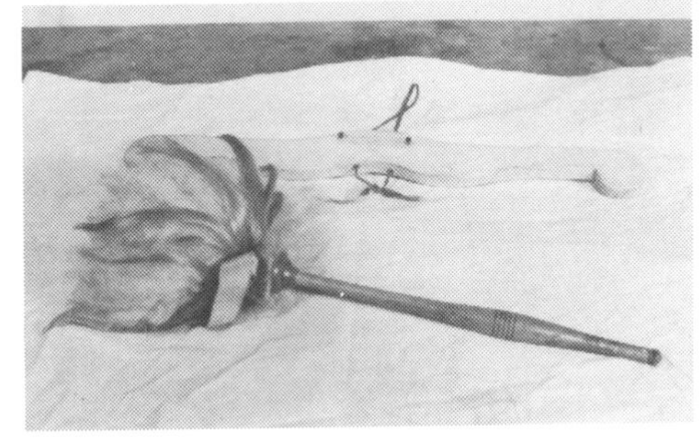

Maple clothes hanger and dusting brush
Hanger signed "Sisters" side," brush has original ribbons.
Value: Hanger - $60-$75.
Brush - $100-$115.

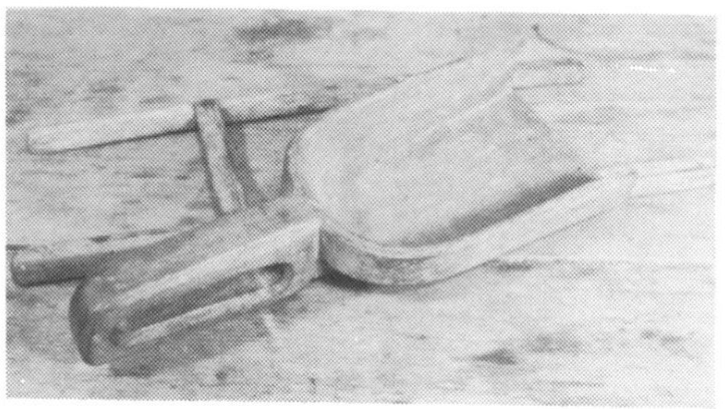

Apple butter scoop
Maple, carved from a single piece of wood, c. 1850.
Value: $200-$225.

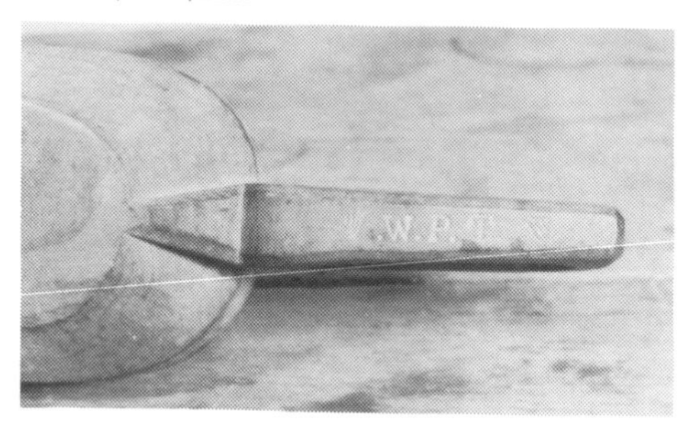

Initials on handle of apple butter scoop

Woven horsehair sieve
New England, great color in woven horsehair, c. 1880.
Value: $100-$125.

Leather sewing kit
Pincushions in both ends; space for needles and buttons, c. 1910.
Value: $85-$100.

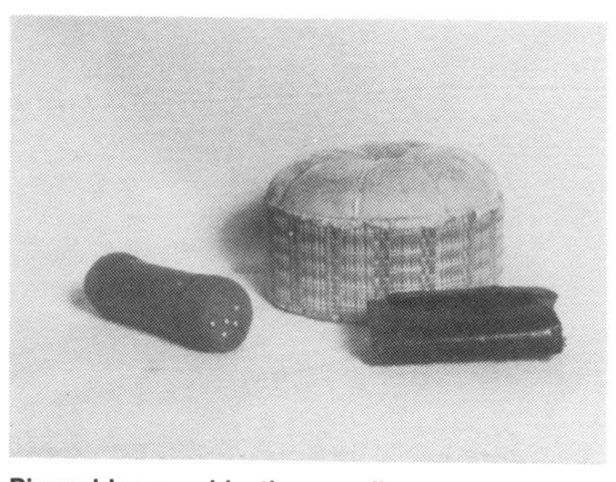

Pincushions and leather needle case
The large pincushion of woven poplar; all three sold in Shaker community shops, c. 1900.
Value: Small pincushion - $30-$40.
Large pincushion - $35-$50.
Leather needle case - $24-$32.

Mount Lebanon seedbox
Lift top, compartmentalized interior, label in excellent condition, c. 1900.
Value: $275-$325.

Shaker seedbox
Pine, New Lebanon, New York, made prior to 1861.
Value: $110-$125 (lid gone).

Shaker Seedbox
Pine, Mount Lebanon, New York, c. 1870s.
Value: $100-$120 (without lid).

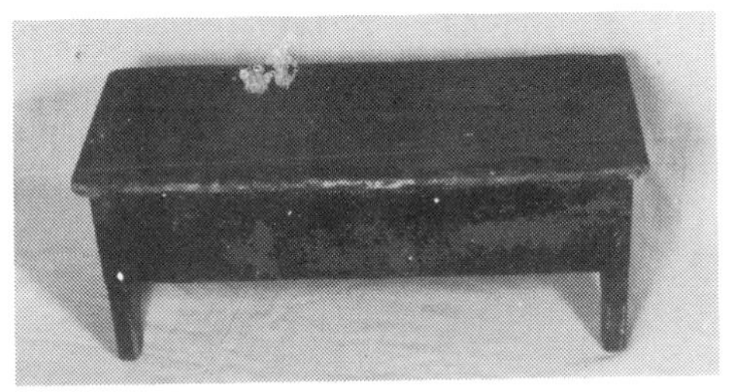

Footstool
Pine, early green paint, worn top, half-moon cutouts, c. 1840.
Value: $125-$135.

Footstool
Replaced tapes, refinished, c. 1880.
Value: $90-$100.

Shaker #3 rocking chair
Replaced tapes, original finish, Mount Lebanon, New York, c. 1880-1890.
Value: $400-$450.

Decal used on slat of Shaker #3 rocker

Shaker #1 rocking chair
Replaced tapes, #1 impressed into rear of top slat, Mount Lebanon, New York, c. 1880-1890.
Value: $500-$575.

Shaker rocking chairs with the Mount Lebanon decal are worth $15-$30 more than chairs without it. The replaced tapes generally do not affect the value of the chair. The chairs with the impressed number on the rear of the top slat and/or a decal were production chairs made for the "world," and not for use in the Shaker communities.

Rocking chair
Replaced tapes, arms with mushroom tenon caps, cushion rail, c. 1880.
Value: $700-$850.

The bar or rail above the top slat was used to tie a back cushion on the chair. In 1876, the cushions sold for $4 each, the chairs for $10.

Armchair
Replaced tapes, original finish, production chair, c. 1880.
Value: $650-$800.

New tapes in the original Shaker designs may be purchased at several of the Shaker restorations.

Shaker armchair
Original splint seat, original finish, not a production chair, c. 1830-1840.
Value: $500-$650.

Shaker drop-front desk
Pine, Enfield, Connecticut, original finish, c. 1850.
Value: $4,000-$5,500.

Close-up
Dovetailed drawer in drop-front desk.

Shaker dry sink
C. 1840.
Value: $1,800-$2,220.

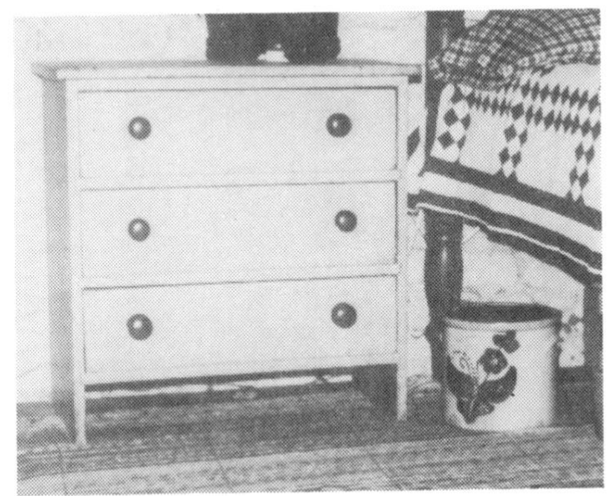

Three-drawer chest
Pine, blue paint, original condition, New England Shaker, c. 1850.
Value: $1,200-$1,500.

Berry bucket or pail
Bail handle, yellow exterior, white interior, staved construction, c. late nineteenth century.
Value: $115-$125.

The bottom of the pail is signed "E.H. No. 10." The iron diamond-shaped braces on the sides of the pail are typical of Shaker construction in staved buckets or pails.

Berry bucket or pail
Staved construction, iron bands, "diamond" braces, 5" diameter, c. late nineteenth century.
Value: $95-$110.

Berry bucket or pail
Staved construction, iron bands, "diamond" braces, deep red paint, c. late nineteenth century.
Value: $95-$110.

Field bucket
Maple handle, blue paint, original condition, staved construction, leather spout, c. 1860.
Value: $330-$375.

Swing handle storage box
Lid, soft red paint, original condition, c. 1870.
Value: $150-$175.

Swing handle box
Copper nails, original unpainted finish, "Hancock, Mass." impressed in bottom, c. 1900.
Value: $95-$115.

Cheese box
Yellow paint, button hoop construction, impressed "Harvard," c. 1860.
Value: $240-$275.

Bucket
Original condition, "diamond" braces, staved construction, unpainted, c. 1900.
Value: $75-$100.

Carrier
Yellow "wash," finger lap construction, maple sides, pine bottom, copper nails, c. 1870.
Value: $385-$425.

Carrier
Finger lap construction, four "fingers," remnants of red stain, c. 1870.
Value: $385-$425.

Back side of Shaker oval box
Yellow paint, "P.C." in red, five fingers, c. 1830.
Value: $550-$650.

In the bottom of the lid of this oval box is the following history:

"Polly Congleton gave this box to Eldress Pauline Bryant when she died Aug. 3, 1833"

In another person's handwriting is the following: "Given me Aug. 1886 by Eldress Pauline Bryant on her death bed.
Pleasant Hill Kentucky"

A provenance or history attached to a Shaker box or piece of furniture adds significantly to its value.

Oval box
Light green paint, four "fingers," copper nails, c. second half of nineteenth century.
Value: $300-$350.

Oval box
Finger lap construction, blue paint, copper nails, c. second half of nineteenth century.
Value: $275-$300.

Oval box
Finger lap construction, bittersweet colored paint, four "fingers," c. second half of nineteenth century.
Value: $500-$600.

Oval box
Finger lap construction, copper nails, two "fingers," 5½" x 3", yellow paint, c. second half of nineteenth century.
Value: $250-$300.

This box appears to have been made by the Harvard, Massachusetts, Shakers.

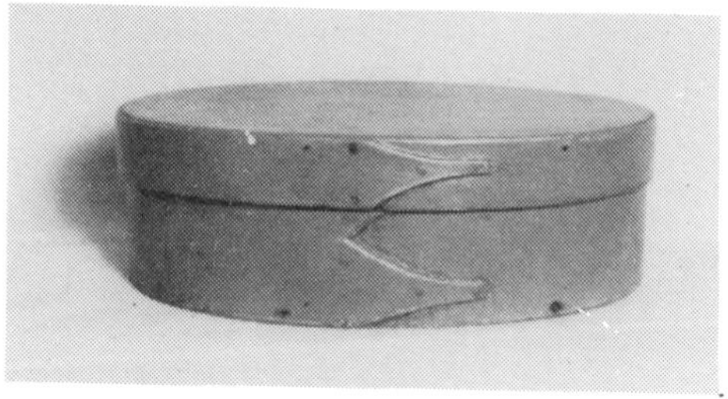

Oval box
Finger lap construction, copper nails, two fingers, blue paint, c. second half of nineteenth century.
Value: $325-$350.

A close look at this box shows part of a third "finger" hidden under the side of the lid. This box could legitimately be advertised as a two-or-three-finger box.

Painted boxes are more eagerly sought after by collectors than unpainted boxes. The bittersweet box at left, and various shades of blue boxes are the most uncommon. A potential buyer of a Shaker box in "original" paint should look carefully for legitimate signs of wear. The two boxes below would have their value increased by at least 50 to 75 percent if they were painted.

Oval boxes
Unpainted original condition, finger lap construction, copper nails, c. second half of nineteenth century.
Value: $185-$210.

Oval boxes
Dark green paint, made by Harvard, Massachusetts, Shakers, c. 1850.
Value: $200-$220.

Compare the fingers in these boxes with the construction techniques of the box above:

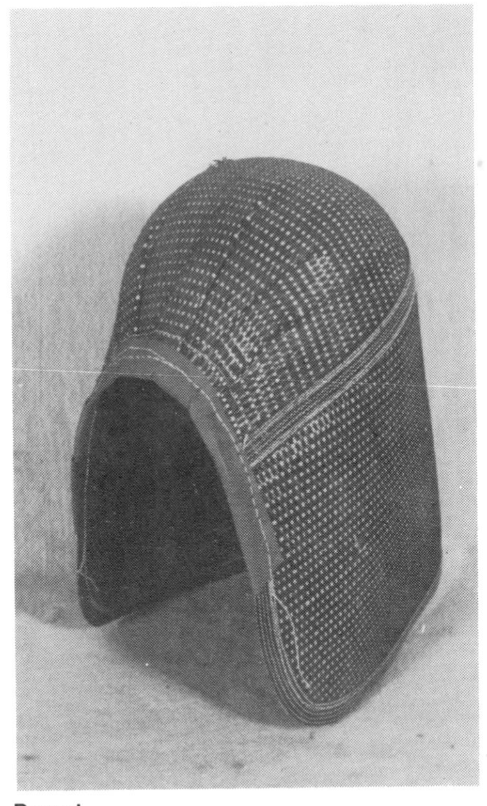

Bonnet
Woven poplar, size #6, c. 1880-1890.
Value: $85-$110.

Bonnet of woven poplar with attached neck shade
C. 1890.
Value: $95-$110.

Bonnet
Woven poplar, c. 1890.
Value: $75-$95.

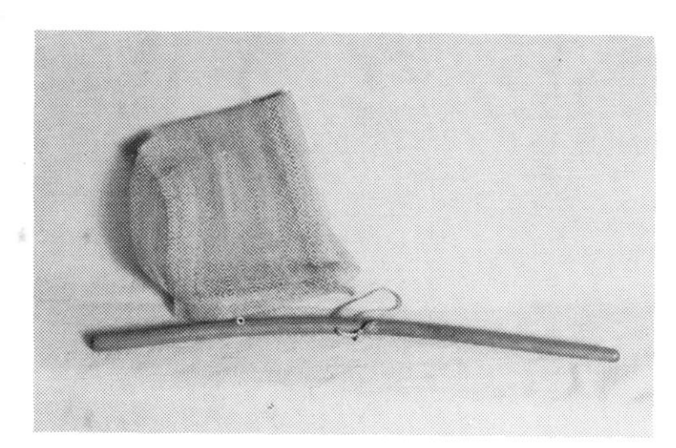

Bonnet and clothes hanger
Summer-weight bonnet, maple hanger, c. 1850.
Value: Hanger - $50-$55
Bonnet - $70-$75.

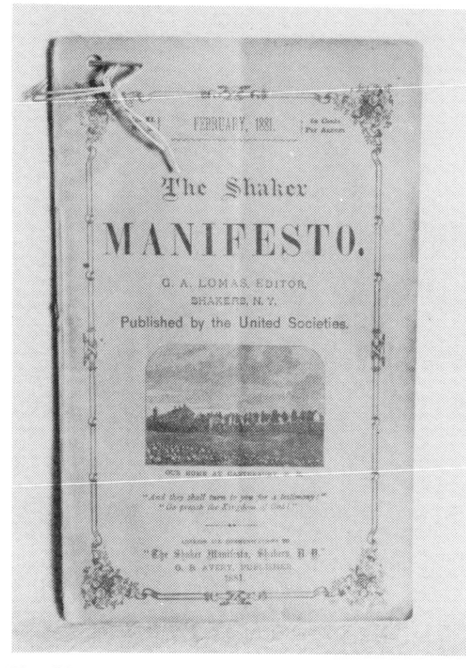

The Shaker Manifesto
Printed between 1871-1900, mint original condition, copy dated 1881.
Value: $35-$45.

Framed Shaker string bean label
Mount Lebanon, New York, great graphics, c. early 1900s.
Value: $65-$75.

Miniature sieve
Original condition, 3″ diameter, woven hair, c. late nineteenth century.
Value: $75-$95.

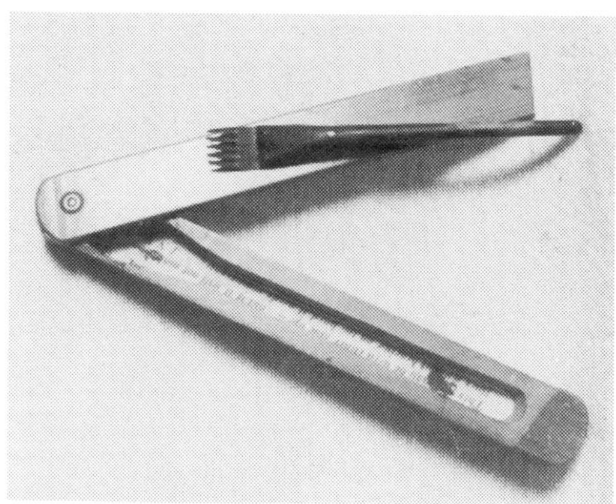

Musical notation pen
Cherry case, five-pointed pen used to draw staff, designed by Isaac Young, c. mid-nineteenth century.
Value: $425-$500.

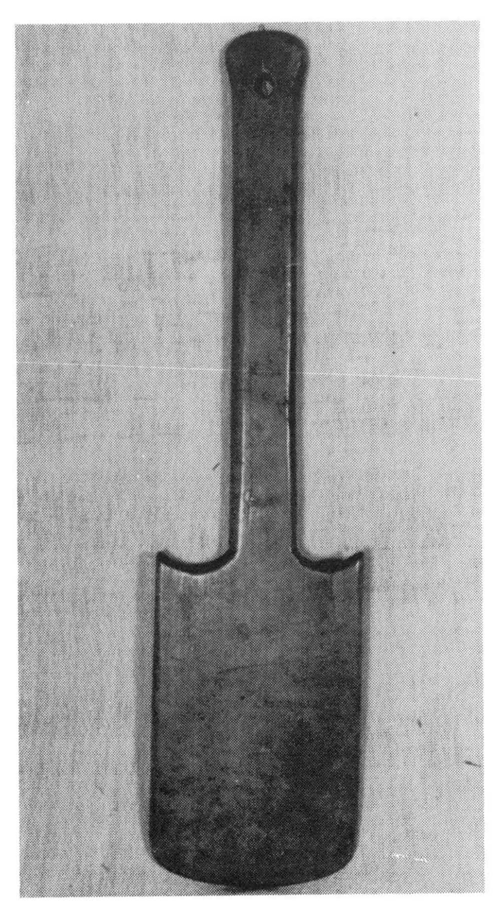

Wooden kitchen utensil
Maple, hand-made, c. 1860
Value: $65-$75.

Clothes scrubber
C. mid-nineteenth century.
Value: $30-$40.

Wooden scoop
Maple, carved from a single piece of wood, c. late nineteenth century.
Value: $85-$100.

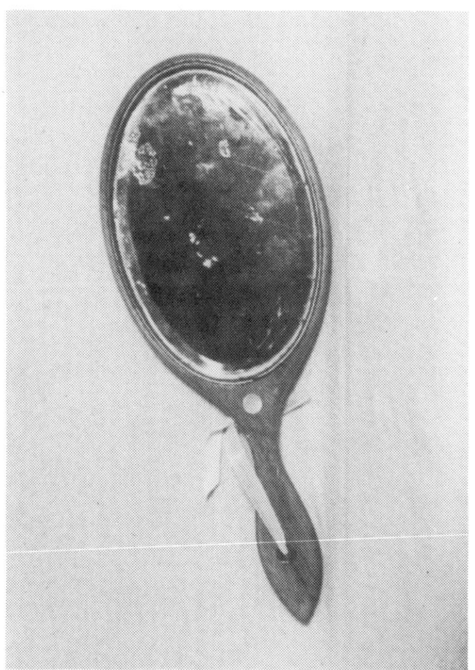

Hand mirror
C. 1860.
Value: $95-$110.

Darning egg
Wooden ball revolves in maple case, c. late nineteenth-early twentieth century.
Value: $50-$65.

Pincushion-spool holder
Turned maple base and stem, made and sold at Sabbathday Lake, Maine, c. twentieth century.
Value: $175-$200.

Sabbathday Lake
Gum-backed label from pincushion.

Tin dustpan
C. late nineteenth century.
Value: $50-$65.

Tin churn
Wooden dasher, tin handles, c. 1860.
Value: $225-$275.

Wooden stirring tool
Used with tin churn, c. 1860.
Value: $40-$45.

Cloak hanger
C. late nineteenth century.
Value: $115-$130.

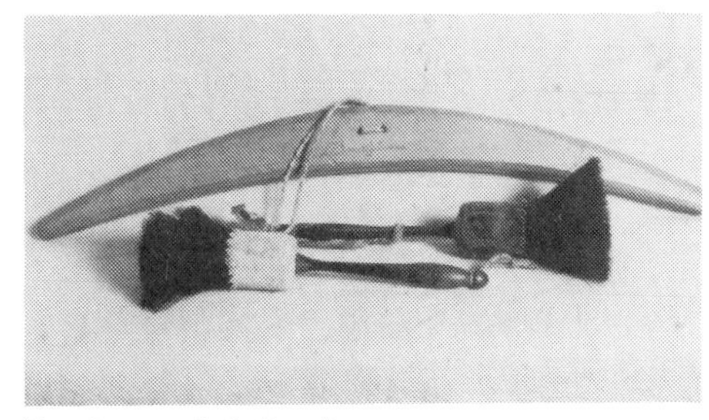

Brushes and clothes hanger
Turned maple handle, colored velvet, maple hanger, c. late nineteenth century.
Value: Brushes - $55-$60.
Hanger - $50 - $55.

Brushes
C. late nineteenth century.
Value: $50-$60.

Brush
Maple handle, red painted metal rim, c. late nineteenth century.
Value: $25-$35.

8 Potpourri

It is extremely difficult to attempt to categorize every aspect of nineteenth and early twentieth century life. We have made an effort to be diligent in identifying and evaluating a myriad of baskets, toys. textiles, Shaker, country furniture, turn-of-the-century furnishings, stoneware, trade signs, and kitchen antiques.

It is important to keep in mind that the prices in this book are "ballpark" estimations that are subject to a wide variety of experiences and potential personal prejudices. We sincerely believe that the wide variety of items discussed and illustrated and the information presented are worth your investment. If any book or price guide prevents you from buying someone else's mistake or provides a firm foundation of knowledge in the purchasing of antiques, the purchase price of the book was money well spent.

We have widened the scope of this edition to include many items that are currently becoming popular among collectors attempting to capture the mythical "country look" that popular magazines are promoting in home decoration.

We have included this section because a number of items pictured and priced here fail to neatly fall in any other chapter.

Trade Signs

Restaurant sign
Found in New Hampshire, green with white lettering, pine, c. 1870-1890.
Value: $325-$350.

Repairman's sign

Pine, white with black lettering, found in southern Illinois, c. 1920-1930.
Value: $100-$115.

A problem with any trade sign used outdoors is weathering damage. This sign borders on the realm of being too rough. It measures 42″ x 22″.

Trade sign

Pine, 13″ x 18″, found in central Illinois, blue with white lettering, c. 1900-1910.
Value: $120-$135.

This is a fairly standard exterior sign. It is not unusual nor exceedingly well executed.

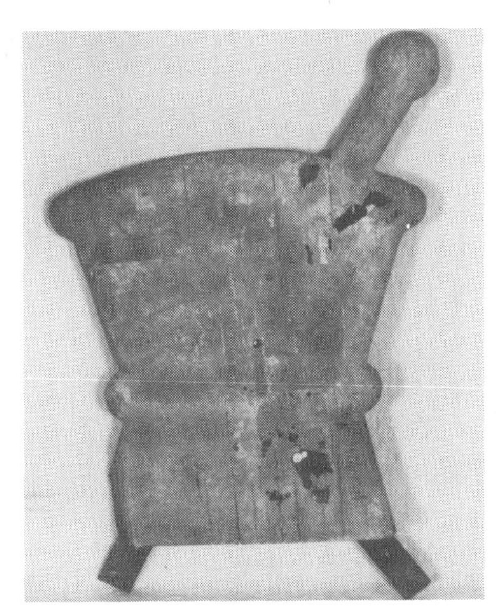

Pharmacy sign
Pine, gold leaf over green paint, 20″ x 14″, c. 1870.
Value: $125-$140.

In 1870, an individual did not have to be able to know that the store at which this sign hung sold laxatives and linament.

Restaurant sign
Found in northern Wisconsin, tin in pine frame, c. 1930.
Value: $145-$165.

Paint sampler
Maple, various colors, decal lettering, interior sign, c. 1880-1900.
Value: $200-$215.

Tavern sign
English, interior sign, c. 1900.
Value: $250-$275.

Shoe store sign
Pine, yellow with black lettering, interior sign, c. 1930-1940.
Value: $50-$60.

Jewelry sign
Cast zinc, black and white, c. 1880.
Value: $150-$175.

Jewelry sign
Cast zinc, gold, white, black lettering, exterior sign. Hands usually set at 8:16 to 8:20, c. 1880.
Value: $175-$200.

Barber shop sign
From Baltimore hotel, copper, brass letters, c. 1900.
Value: $350-$375.

Physician's sign
From Fairbury, Illinois, tin, black with gold lettering, exterior sign, c. 1875.
Value: $60-$70.

Tin sign
New England, black and white lettering, interior sign, c. 1900.
Value: $70-$80.

Town line sign
Cast aluminum, gray with black lettering, c. 1940.
Value: $55-$65.

Dressmaker's sign
Tin, stenciled gold letters on black background, c. 1880.
Value: $65-$75

Poultry sign
Pine, 6′6″ long, c. early 1900s.
Value: $125-$140.

"Closed" sign
Pine, c. 1920s
Value: $55-$70.

It is interesting to note that the owner of the shop never reopened his business at 7 o'clock. The more you get involved in collecting antiques, the more regularly you see this sign.

Odds and Ends

Windmill weight
Cast-iron cow, base added, found in Nebraska, c. 1900.
Value: $135-$150.

Cast-iron display boot from shoe store
Gold boot, red buttons, black heel, c. 1880-1890.
Value: $75-$95.

Cast-iron hitching horse
New horses are being cast from old molds and allowed to weather, c. 1970
Value: $25-$30
Old example - $200-$250.

Whirligig
Carved pine, Union soldier, new base, c. 1870-1900.
Value: $350-$425.

Apothecary chest, c. 1850, $1,750-$2,000

Miniature chest, $350-$400, American pewter, $300-$500

Low-post maple bed, Pennsylvania, c. 1840, $850-$950
Trundle bed, maple, c. 1850, $400-$475

Jelly cupboard, pine, refinished, $450-$550

Cross-section of country antiques

Cloth doll, late nineteenth century, $250-$275

Tavern table, $475-$525; chairs, $385 (l), $275 (r)

Pine cradle, c. 1830s, $650-$700

Rocking horse, c. 1880s, $2,500-$3,500

Garden Baskets, $85-$150

Buckets and firkins, late nineteenth century, $50-$150

Carved grasshopper
Pine, worn paint, tool marks, possibly a trade sign, c. 1870.
Value: $300-$375.

Harness bells
Nickel-plated brass bells, leather strap, c. 1890-1900.
Value: $75-$95.

School bell
Maple handle, brass bell, c. early 1900s, 7½" diameter.
Value: $75-$85.

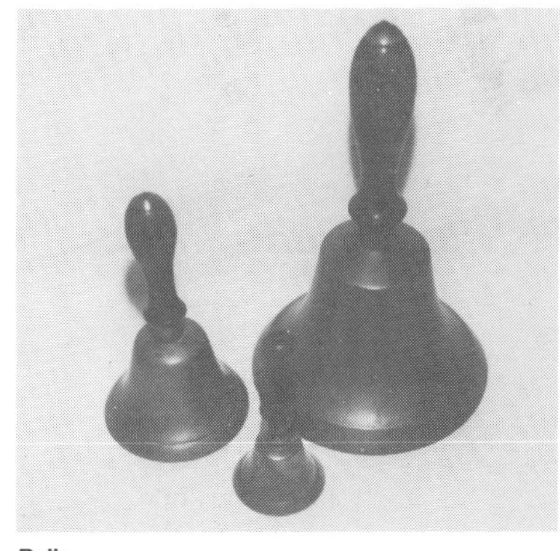

Bells
Maple handled brass bell, c. early 1900s.
Value: $45-$55
(l-r) $30-$40
$60-$75

Cast sundial
C. early 1900s.
Value: $60-$70.

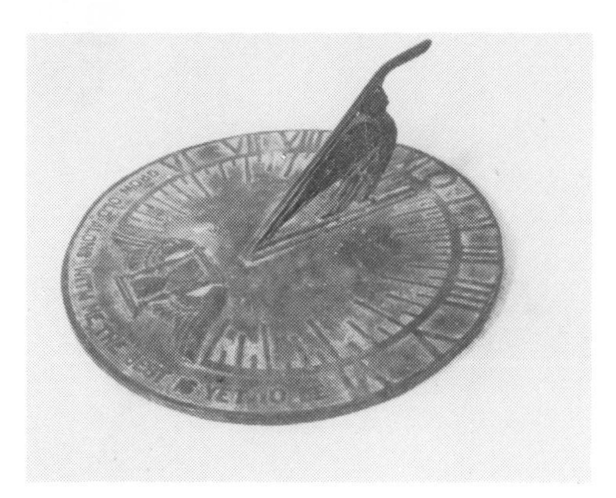

Cast sundial
C. 1900.
Value: $60-$75.

Tin mousetrap
C. 1860.
Value: $24-$28.

Carved straight razor
Tin blade, maple handle, found in New York State, c. 1870.
Value: $65-$70.

Printed birth certificate
Pennsylvania, hand watercolored, c. 1845.
Value: $95-$110.

Copper stencil
Used in Crystal Spring Creamery, c. 1880.
Value: $18-$22.

Checkerboard
Pine, red, black and white paint, c. 1900-1910.
Value: $115-$130.

Store pepper container
Holds 100 pounds, maple top, paper sides, c. 1880.
Value: $75-$85.

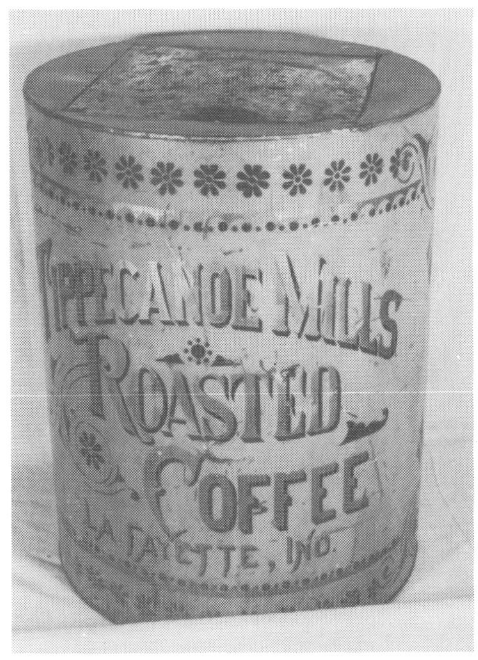

Roasted coffee store container
C. 1880.
Value: $120-$140.

Seedbox (interior)
C. 1900.
Value: $115-$125.

Seedbox (exterior)

Seedbox
C. late nineteenth century.
Value: $135-$150.

The quality and color of the exterior and interior labels are the primary value determinant of non-Shaker seedboxes.

Seedbox
C. 1900.
Value: $85-$100

Seedbox
Pine, c. 1890.
Value: $135-$150.

Seedbox
Oak, c. 1920.
Value: $50-$65.

Mustard boxes
C. 1900.
Value: $50-$60
$55-$70

Grocery box
C. early 1900s.
Value: $50-$55

Doll cradle
Walnut, heart cutout, early red paint, c. 1830.
Value: $115-$130.

Egg crate
Used for carrying four dozen eggs, pine, painted blue, c. early 1900s.
Value: $75-$85.

Wooden cannon
Gold gun, blue carriage, red trim, c. 1880.
Value: $175-$200.

Coca-Cola carton
Pine, tin advertisement, c. 1940.
Value: $18-$25.

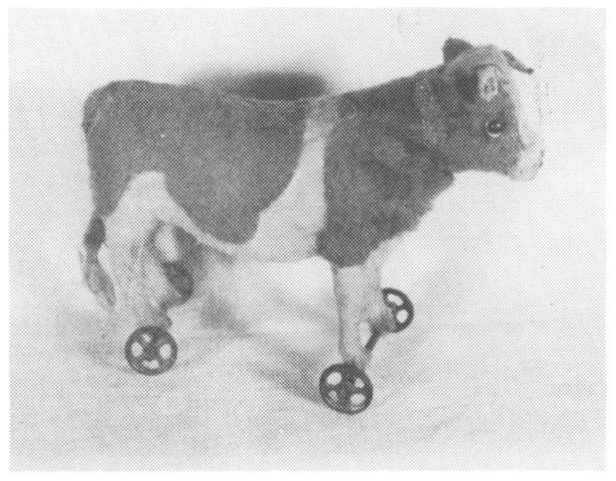

Toy cow
Cast-iron wheels, brown and white fur, c. 1900.
Value: $150-$175.

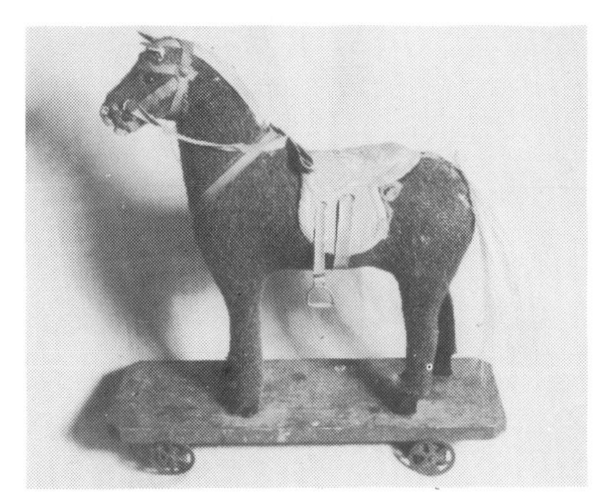

Child's pull-toy horse
C. 1900.
Value: $85-$100.

Cast-iron railroad car
C. 1920.
Value: $30-$35.

Cast-iron cat bank, block box, ball
C. 1900-1915.
Value: Iron cat - $35-$40.
Ball - $12-$14.
Block box - $15-$18.

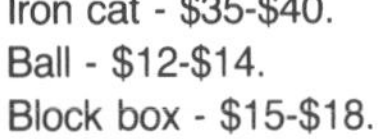

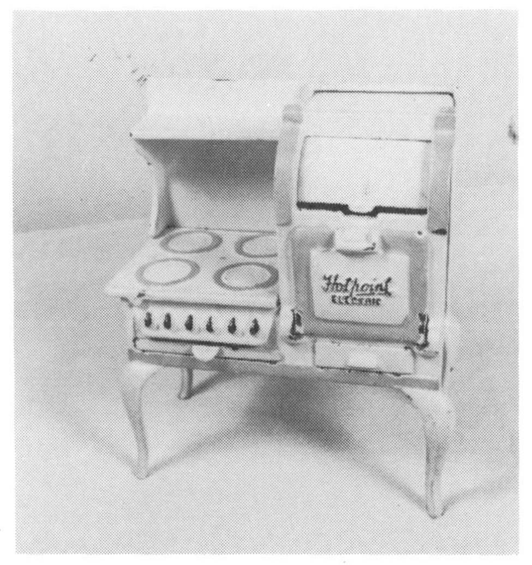

Hotpoint child's stove
C. 1930-1940.
Value: $75-$90.

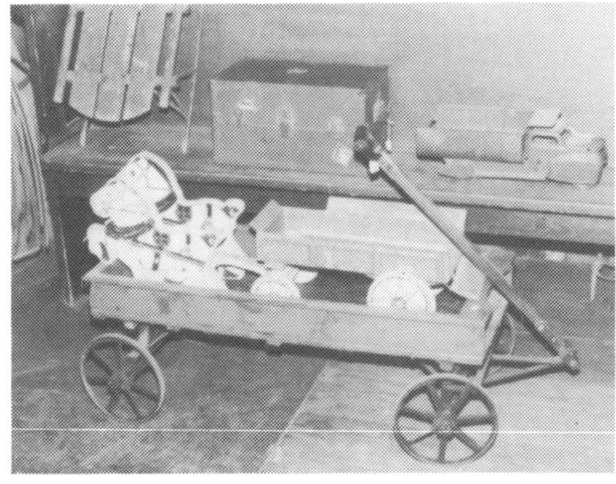

Wooden wagon
Pine, iron wheels, c. 1940.
Value: $35-$45.

Glass marbles
C. early 1900s.
Value: $.50-$35.

Child's pitcher and bowl set
Tin, c. 1900-1910.
Value: $85-$100.

Child's alphabet blocks
Pine, worn condition, c. 1915.
Value: Individual blocks — $1-$2.
Set of twenty-six, worn condition — $40-$50.
Set of twenty-six mint condition — $100-$125.

Black dolls
C. early 1900s
Values: $45, $75, $80

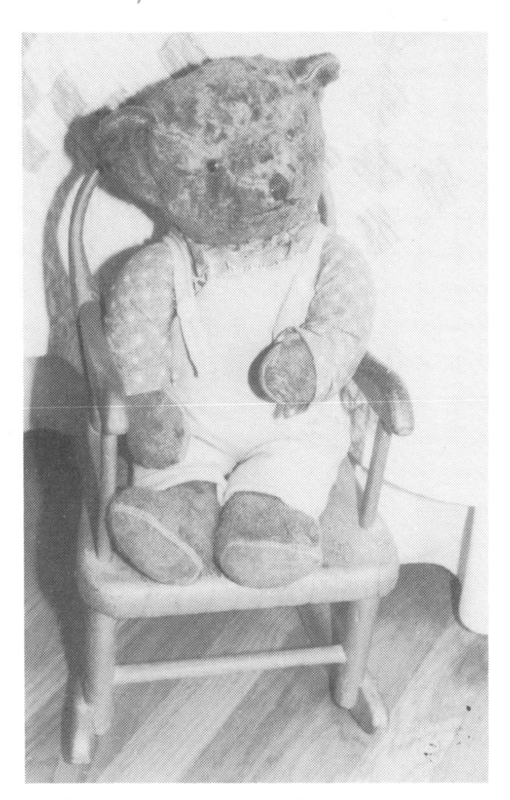

Teddy bear and rocking chair
C. 1910-1920.
Value: Bear — $80-$100.
Chair — $75-$90.

Black dolls
Variety of forms, c. 1880-1900.
Value: $75-$200.

Comb box with mirror
Impressed decoration, oak, c. 1900.
Value: $75-$85.

Seth Thomas kitchen clock
C. early 1900s.
Value: $200-$225.

Seth Thomas mantel clock
C. 1850s.
Value: $200-$225.

Walnut pillar clock
C. 1885-1900.
Value: $125-$150.

Duck decoy
Pine, original paint, unsigned, c. early 1900s.
Value: $65-$75.

Cast iron doorstop
C. 1900
Value: $60-$75.

Dog doorstop
Cast iron, c. early 1900s.
Value: $55-$65.

Wheelbarrow
Pine, painted red, c. 1930s-1940s.
Value: $55-$75.

Wine press
C. 1930s
Value: $60-$80

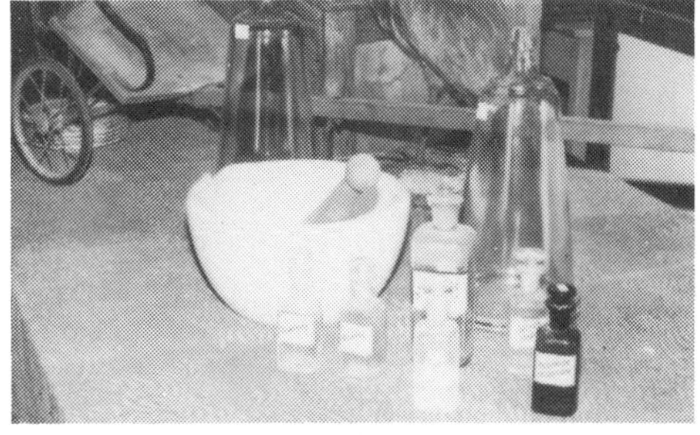

Pharmacist's mortar and pestle
C. early 1900s
Value: $75-$95.

Fire extinguishers
C. 1930s-1940s.
Value: $10-$12 each.

Wooden toy biplane
C. 1930-1940.
Value: $30-$35.

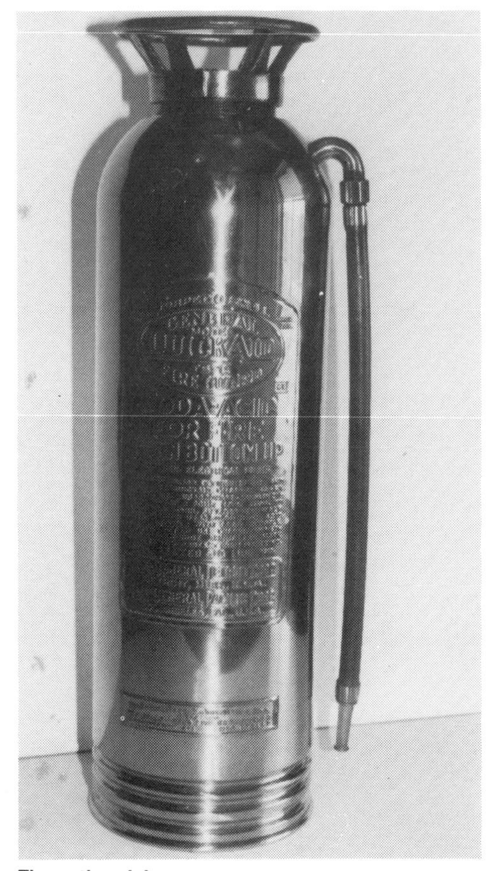

Fire extinguisher
Burnished copper, brass label, c. 1930s.
Value: $80-$90.

Edison phonograph
Decorated horn, working condition, oak case, c. 1900-1905.
Value: $550-$700.

Ansonia music box
C. 1870s.
Value: $500-$550.

Daguerreotypes
Mid-nineteenth century.
Value: $20 to several hundred.

The value of individual daguerreotypes is largely determined by the uniqueness of the subject of the pictures. The incredible increase in prices of anything related to early photography has dramatically changed the market for daguerreotypes.

Textiles

Framed sampler
Early maple frame, dated 1872, "Jane Ann Dunn."
Value: $225-$250.

Sampler
Memorial to Mary Laing, dated 1847.
Value: $200-$240.

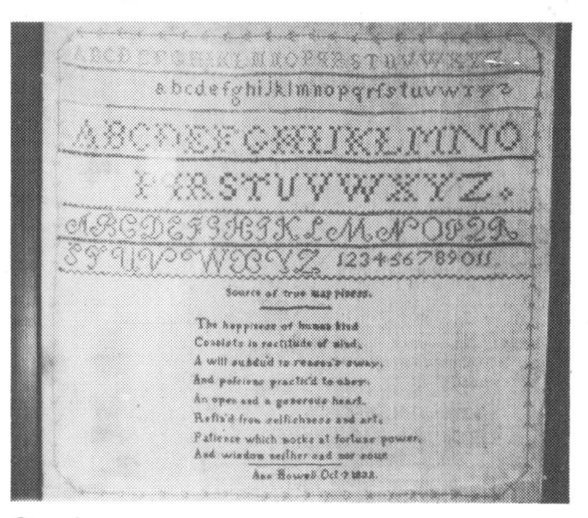

Sampler
Dated 1832.
Value: $160-$175.

Sampler
Roster of family, not dated, c. 1860.
Value: $175-$200.

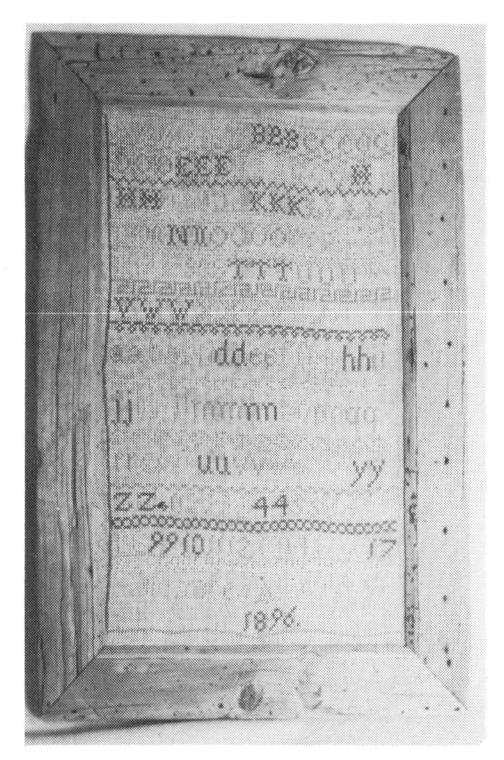

Sampler
Unsigned, dated 1896, late date for a sampler.
Value: $115-$125.

Quilts and Coverlets

Two-color quilt
Variation of the "Lady of the Lake" pattern, type of quilt that provides utility with a minimum of quilting.
Value: $180-$220.

Nine-patch utility quilt
Value: $150-$175.

This is another example of a utility quilt that does not have significant value. Quilts of this type do have added value if the fabric pieces that make up the quilt are of special interest or quality.

Quilt
Unquilted top, "Star of Le Moyne" pattern.
Value: $125-$150.

"Cockscomb Star" quilt
Trapunto feather wreaths and trailing border.
Value: $450-$500.

The great increase in interest in quilting in the 1970s gave rise to some pricing patterns in the early 1980s. Prices on the West Coast and the East Coast are considerably higher than in the Middle West. Many fine examples may still be found in blanket chests and occasional farm sales in Indiana, Missouri, Iowa, Kentucky and Illinois.

Quilt
A variety of patterns.
Value: $275-$300.

This example appears to contain examples of the "Juniper Star" pattern, "Job's Trouble" and "V" blocks at the corners. This is not a common pattern.

Quilt
Nine-patch pierced quilt from Fairbury, Illinois.
Value: $175-$200.

"Baskets of Flowers" utility quilt
Pierced variation of the lily or tulip design.
Value: $210-$240.

Jacquard coverlet
Possibly for a child due to small size, produced from a pattern book, c. 1850.
Value: $200-$225.

Overshot coverlet
New York State, c. 1830.
Value: $250-$275.

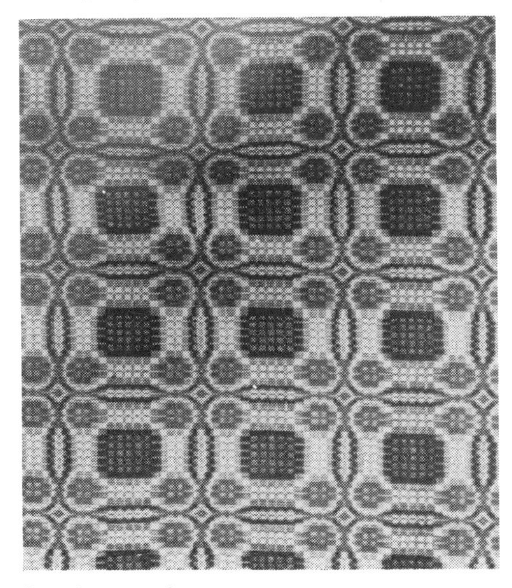

Overshot coverlet
New York State, c. 1830.
Value: $240-$280.

Overshot coverlet
New York State, C. 1850.
Value: $185-$220.

Jacquard coverlet
New York State, c. 1840.
Value: $285-$325.

Crib quilt
"Crazy quilt" pattern, c. 1880-1900.
Value: $80-$100.

9 Trends

On December 27, 1979, an antiques auction in Guernsey, Iowa, typified what collectors in the Midwest and West search for enthusiastically. The majority of the furniture sold was the late Victorian walnut or oak made between 1870 and 1920.

The Guernsey sale included the following pieces:

Walnut

Refinished three-drawer chest, carved pulls - $220.
In-the-rough commode - $100.
Fainting couch that opened to a bed - $100.
Fruit-carved love seat - $340.
Round, revolving top, 60″ poker table - $475.

Oak

Secretary-bookcase, curved glass (two) - $350 and $400.
Kitchen cabinet - $480.
Press-back chairs - $55 to $75 each.
Barber's cabinet - $100.
Square table - $200.
Four-stack bookcase - $225.
Old telephones - $100 and up.
Round dining tables - $400 and up.
Tall-top wardrobe - $160.

It is important to note that the antiques market in these areas thrives on merchandise similar to the type listed above. It is difficult to collect redware, painted furniture, or Bennington pottery when you have never been exposed to it or had the opportunity to purchase it. Collectors of late Victoriana and oak would rather pay $55 to $75 for a pressback chair in rough condition than $1,200 to $2,000 for a fan-back Windsor chair. The Windsor would not fit in with their other furnishings and they might be forced to drive 1,000 miles before they could begin to see country and New England antiques of this type in any kind of quantity.

Collectors in many states west of Ohio who are interested in early pieces seldom have the opportunity to attend auctions or shows or visit shops where country antiques may be purchased.

If a dower chest or chair table had been handed down in a family for two centuries and quietly emerged at an auction in Guernsey it would very probably sell for considerably less than at an auction in Binghamton, New York, or Concord, New Hampshire.

On November 27, 1979, an auction was held in Sterling, Massachusetts, that included a number of pieces that collectors in Guernsey, Iowa, would have fought over. An oak sideboard with a "mirror and a fancy carved crest with a lion's head" brought $250. An oak china closet with a bow front and curved glass was also purchased for $250. A press-back oak highchair with a caned seat sold for $135. An oak side-by-side (china cabinet and desk) was bid up to $275.

On December 5, 1979, in Shrewsbury, Massachusetts, the following pieces of oak furniture sold at auction:

Mission desk with leaded sliding glass doors - $260.
Gingerbread clock with pressed leaf design - $90.
Gingerbread calendar clock - $130.
Round oak table - $250.

It is impossible to draw accurate conclusions and to make generalizations based on the information from two auctions in the East and one in the Midwest. The conclusions we are tempted to draw are based on personal experience and observation. The auctions serve to substantiate trends we have observed for the past several years. Prices on particular types and periods of furniture fluctuate considerably in different sections of the country. The market presently for oak and turn-of-the-century collectibles is much greater in the Midwest and on the West Coast than in New England. The reverse is the case for country furniture, yet the trend may be changing gradually.

We see the demand for New England and country antiques across the nation growing steadily. This may be due to an increasing awareness by the print media. *Country Living, Colonial Homes, House Beautiful, Good Housekeeping, Early American Life* and many major newspapers feature regular articles and colored pictures of homes furnished with painted furniture, quilts, baskets, and decorated stoneware.

There is no question that prices for factory-produced oak in the Eastern states are extremely reasonable when judged by Midwestern and Far Western standards. It is still possible for Eastern dealers to make profitable trips to California with loads of oak. The oak is typically easier to find in *quantity* in New York State and New England than are country antiques. The dealer in country pieces and accessories must spend a great deal of money and time on the road to fill up his truck. It is impossible to find quality merchandise in quantity in a limited geographic area at reasonable prices that allow for a profit margin large enough to make frequent trips worthwhile.

We have included a wide variety of late nineteenth century and early twentieth century pottery, lighting, furniture, and kitchen antiques to gain some perspective on price trends. The prices for furniture and accessories of this period will certainly rise and fall as one travels east or west from Middle America.

Icebox
Oak, c. 1880-1910, original hardware.
Value: $375-$425.

Wardrobe
Oak. c. 1880-1890, two drawers below, "knockdown" type.
Value: $650-$700.

Cupboard
Oak. c. 1880-1895, pressed floral decoration.
Value: $450-$500.

The circular cutouts at the base of the cupboard were originally covered with screen wire and the section was used much like a pie safe for storing baked goods and food.

Kitchen cabinet
Oak, c. 1900, signed Wilson & Co.
Value: $350-$425.

Kitchen cabinets of this type provided a zinc covered work area, lined storage drawers for flour and sugar, and a glazed area above for dishes and crockery.

Round dining table
Oak, two leaves, c. 1880-1900.
Value: $375-$425.

Commode
Oak, c. 1890, towel bar.
Value: $275-$300.

Tea cart
Walnut c. early 1900s.
Value: $200-$225.

Table
Walnut, c. 1880.
Value: $175-$200.

Close-up
Impressed back of the oak dining chairs.

Dining chairs
Oak, impressed decoration, cane seats, spindle-back, hip rests, c. 1885.
Value: $140-$160 each.
Set of four in similar condition — $775-$800.

Dining chairs
Walnut, cane seat, impressed decoration, c. 1880.
Value: $115-$125,
Set of four in similar condition — $575-$600.

Close-up
Impressed decoration on the dining chairs.

Dining chairs
Maple, cane seats, hip rests, impressed decoration, c. 1875-1885.
Value: $115-$125.

Child's rocking chair
Maple, impressed decoration, spindle-back, c. early 1900s.
Value: $85-$110.

Rocking chair
Oak, spindle-back, impressed decoration, c. 1890.
Value: $185-$210.

Armchair
Walnut, Eastlake style, impressed decoration, c. 1875.
Value: $290-$325.

Side chair and candle stand
Walnut, Eastlake style, impressed decoration, c. 1870.
Value: Side chair — $250-$275.
Candle stand — $150-$175.

"Gingerbread" Clock
Oak, impressed decoration, designed for a mantel, sold by turn-of-the-century mail order houses, c. 1900.
Value: $120-$135.

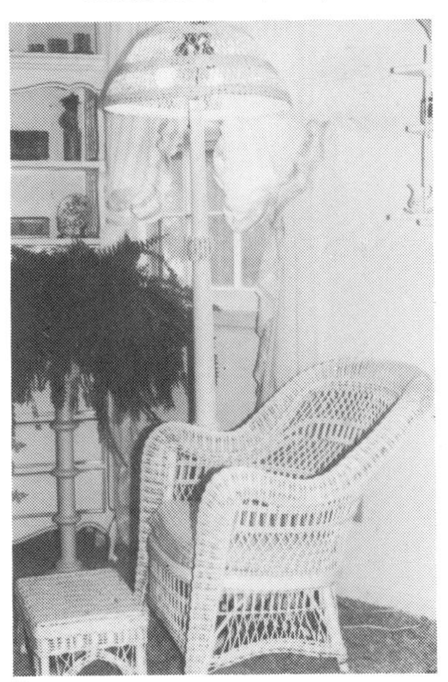

Wicker porch chair and lamp
Willow, c. 1915-1920.
Value: Chair — $140-$155.
Lamp — $400-$450.
Footstool — $55-$65.

Wall telephone
Oak, c. 1930.
Value: $100-$125.

Yarn picture
Handcrafted walnut frame, dated 1894, from the Springer family of Stanford, Illinois.
Value: $250-$275.

Quilt rack
Mahogany, c. 1880.
Value: $85-$95.

Steamer trunk
Pine frame, covered with leather, interior papered, lift-out drawer and storage box, found in original condition, c. 1910.
Value: $75-$90.

Dining chairs
Walnut, cane seats, half-spindle backs, refinished, c. 1875-1890.
Value: $115-$130 each.
$800-$850 set of four.

Sewing or nursing rocking chair
Walnut, cane seat and back, c. 1875-1890.
Value: $135-$150.

Walnut kitchen cupboard
Glazed front, c. 1870s.
Value: $750-$875.

Walnut cupboard
Unusual galley with shelf, used as a storage piece, c. 1870s.
Value: $600-$750.

Meat block
Sycamore, factory-made, maple legs, c. 1920s-1930s.
Value: $375-$425.

We used to almost trip over meat blocks in our travels but they have now almost disappeared. Many states now have regulations that limit their use in grocery stores or meat markets.

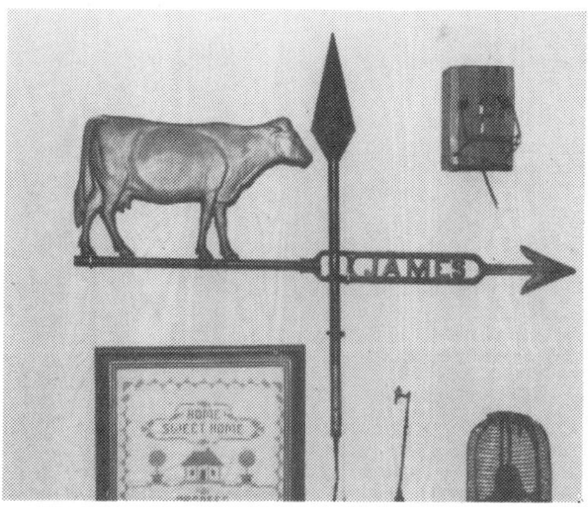

Cow weathervane
Cast zinc, c. 1920.
Value: $95-$115.

Cross-section of kitchen utensils
From the early 1900s.
Value: $6-$35.

These are the types of early twentieth century kitchen utensils that are becoming popular in decorating a "country" kitchen. They are available in such quantities that they are still inexpensive and commonly found almost anywhere. A Sears-Roebuck catalog from the 1900-1930 period can date almost all of them.

Portable toilet
Pine, hinged lid, c. late nineteenth century.
Value: $50-$75 (without chamber pot).

This example preceded the type you see by construction sites by almost a century. Note the great patina on the seat.

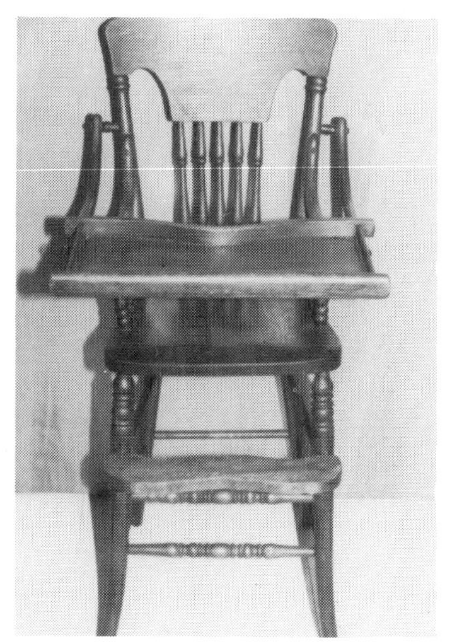

Highchair
Oak, spindle-back, c. 1880-1900.
Value: $140-$150.

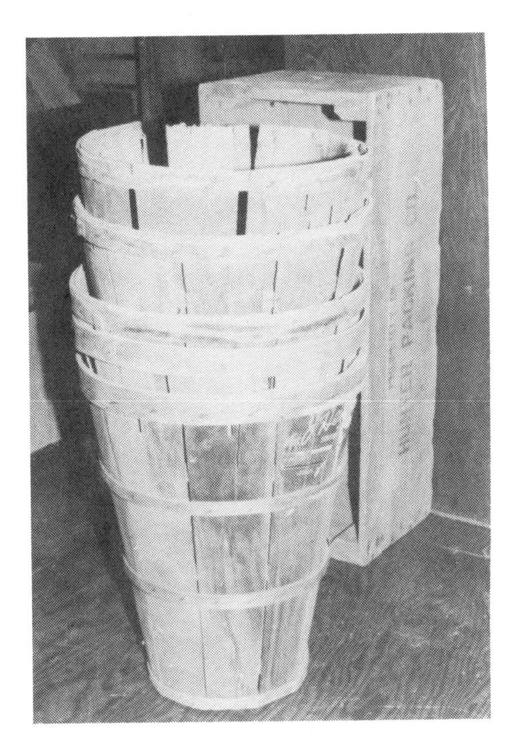

Orchard baskets
Factory-constructed, stapled bands, c. 1940s.
Value: $1-$3.

The thickness and width of the splint used in the construction of a basket is a key to its age. These baskets were mass-produced and held together by staples and ash bands.

Shopping basket
Factory-made, c. 1940s
Value: $10-$12

The bottom of this basket contains wide and thick pieces of splint. Note the regularity of the over-and-under woven splint. Each piece is identical because they were turned out by a verneering machine.

Stoneware spittoon
Molded, sponge-decorated, c. 1880-1890.
Value: $75-$85.

Chamber pot
Molded, sponge-decorated, c. 1880-1890, originally part of a set with a pitcher and bowl.
Value: $65-$75.

Collection of stoneware pitchers
Molded, c. 1880-1910.
Value: $50-$80.

Midwestern stoneware crocks and jugs
C. late nineteenth century-early twentieth century.
Value: $8-$25.

This is the type of stoneware that is commonly available to most collectors in many antiques shops. It does not carry cobalt decoration because it was produced in the dying days of the American stoneware industry.

Pitcher and bowl
Molded, stoneware, unmarked (unsigned), c. 1880-1890.
Value: $75-$100.

Two-gallon crock
Stenciled decoration, Western Stoneware Co., Monmouth, Illinois, c. 1900-1915.
Value: $20-$25.

Advertising containers
C. 1900-1930.
Value: $10-$30.

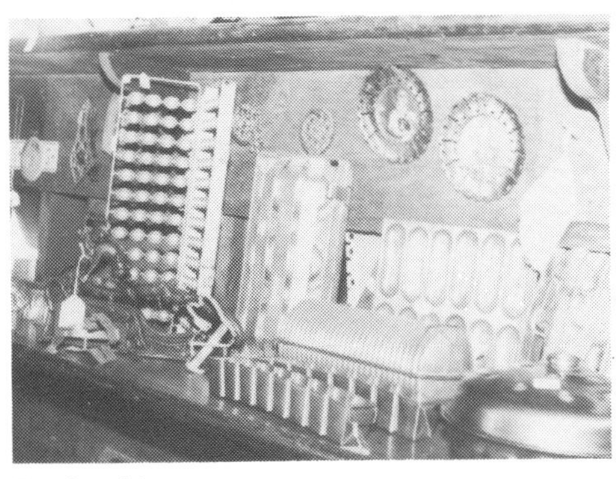

Food molds
C. 1930s.
Value: $12-$35.

Advertising Containers
C. 1930s-1940s
Values: $8-$18.

10 Final Examination II

In the first edition of this book we took pity on the readers and presented questions that almost anyone off the street could have answered. This quiz is a little more difficult and many of you will have to stretch to score well. Keep in mind that this is probably one of the most critical moments of your life. If you do not want to humiliate yourself, close the book.

If you have foolishly chosen to continue, read each question carefully and choose the most appropriate response. You can then check your answers for accuracy on page 206.

1. (True) (False) The interior of this crock was colored a chocolate brown with Utica slip.

2. This crock dates from about
   a. 1840.
   b. 1860.
   c. 1880.
   d. could be any of the above.

3. (True) (False) This crock is worth *at least* $210.

4. The decoration on this crock was
   a. impressed.
   b. incised.
   c. slip-trailed.
   d. none of the above.

5. (True) (False) This piece of stoneware was molded rather than hand thrown.

6. (True) (False) This crock is worth *at least* $210.

7. Estimate the approximate date of this spice chest.

8. Its approximate value is ____________.

9. If the spice chest had been repainted, what would be its approximate value?
   a. less.
   b. considerably less.
   c. about the same.

10. This basket is made of
    a. ash splint.
    b. rye straw.
    c. oak splint.
    d. could be any of the above.
    e. none of the above.

11. The constructon of this basket may be described as
    a. coiled.
    b. plaited.
    c. ribbed.
    d. checker worked.

12. The fruit jars are
    a. filled with applesauce.
    b. filled with tomatoes.
    c. filled with green beans.
    d. filled with pickle relish.
    e. all of the above.

13. This lantern is
    a. a rare piece of early lighting.
    b. an import.
    c. *at least* 150 years old.
    d. all of the above.

14. The light source in this lantern was
    a. whale oil.
    b. kerosene.
    c. a candle.
    d. electricity.

15. The approximate value of this lantern is
    a. $400.
    b. $300.
    c. $200.
    d. less than $100.

16. This crock is worth
    a. $150.
    b. $250.
    c. more than $250.

17. (True) (False) The decoration on this crock was stenciled.

18. What would the value of this six-gallon crock be without the bird and floral decoration?
    a. less than $50.
    b. more than $50 but less than $100.
    c. more than $100.

19. This is a
    a. settle.
    b. wagon seat.
    c. settee.
    d. deacon's bench.
20. The seat is made of
    a. rush.
    b. cane.
    c. splint.
    d. woven cloth or tape.
21. This piece probably dates from the ______ ______ period.
    a. 1740-1760
    b. 1830-1840
    c. 1800-1820
    d. 1870-1890

22. This piece of woodenware is made of
    a. burl.
    b. walnut.
    c. pine.
    d. maple.
23. The __________ is used to grind up whatever is placed in the __________ .

24. What type of ladder is this?
    a. paint ladder
    b. meat ladder
    c. fire ladder
    d. just a ladder
    e. orchard ladder

25. This measure was constructed by the
    a. Shakers.
    b. Pennsylvania Dutch.
    c. Zoarites.
    d. Quakers.

26. The nails or tacks used in the construction of this measure were
    a. copper.
    b. iron.
    c. brass.
    d. made in Europe and imported into the U.S. by the Pilgrims.

27. The purpose of the "finger" or "lapper" was to ______________________________
    ______________________________.

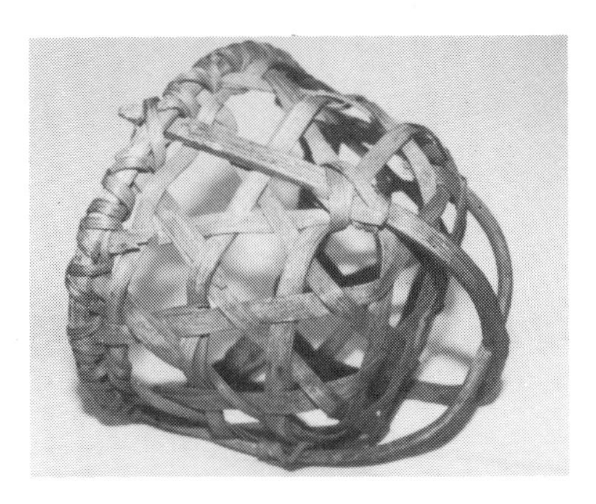

28. This is a
    a. feed basket.
    b. ox muzzle.
    c. cheese drainer.
    d. curd basket.

29. How would you date this "Hand-E-Washboard"?
    Circa ________________ .

Match the definitions with the proper terms

____ 30. "lights"
____ 31. demijohn bottom
____ 32. scribe
____ 33. snipe hinge
____ 34. till
____ 35. incised

a. a small box inside a blanket chest
b. two distinct pieces of furniture that have been joined to form a single piece
c. "kicked in"
d. a tool used by a joiner to mark where various cuts or holes were to be made in a piece of furniture
e. cotter pin
f. a method of decorating stoneware
g. glass

---

36. The correct chronology of the manner in which stoneware was decorated was

a. stencil, slip cup, impressed.
b. slip cup, stencil, brush painting.
c. neither of the above is correct.

Match the author with their area of expertise

____ 37. woodenware
____ 38. furniture
____ 39. lighting

a. Alan I. Weintraub
b. Mary Earle Gould
c. Robert Keller
d. Arthur Hayward
e. Wallace Nutting
f. Barry Spitznass

40. (True) (False) The purpose of the breadboard end is to keep the three-board top from warping.

41. The bird on this crock was
    a. stenciled.
    b. incised.
    c. impressed.
    d. none of the above.

42. The potter's mark was
    a. incised.
    b. impressed.
    c. neither of the above.

43. This crock dates from about
    a. the 1840s.
    b. the 1860s.
    c. the 1870s.
    d. the 1970s.

44. The top of this bench is ____________ to the base.
    a. mortised
    b. dovetailed
    c. pinned
    d. butted up

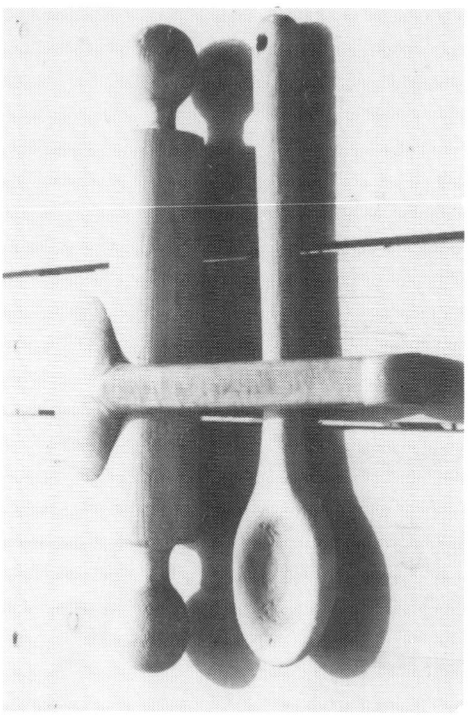

45. (True) (False) The three examples illustrated here could also be called treenware.

46. This is a ____________-back chair.
    a. bannister
    b. slat
    c. ladder
    d. none of the above
    e. b + c

47. The seat of the chair is
    a. rush.
    b. splint.
    c. cane.
    d. taped.

48. What does this chair *not* have
    a. finials.
    b. stretchers.
    c. a rush seat.
    d. all of the above.
    e. none of the above.

49. If two inches had been added to the height of the chair legs, it would have been
    a. pieced out.
    b. married.
    c. neither of the above.

50. The lines on the back post of this chair are called ____________________________.

Answers

1. False — Albany slip
2. c
3. False
4. d
5. False
6. False
7. 1880-1910 is probably a good estimate.
8. $95-$115
9. The value of this chest is primarily found in its original condition.
10. b
11. a
12. Call this a Christmas gift.
13. b
14. c
15. d — Considerably less than $100.
16. c
17. False
18. a
19. b
20. c
21. b
22. d
23. Pestle, mortar
24. b — The ladder was hung in front of the hearth horizontally between two beams and meat was tied to the ladder.
25. a
26. a
27. Control the expansion and contraction of the wood.
28. b
29. Some point between 1900 and 1920.
30. g
31. c
32. d
33. e
34. a
35. f
36. c
37. b
38. e
39. d
40. True
41. d
42. b
43. d (It is a reproduction.)
44. a
45. True
46. e
47. b
48. c
49. a
50. Scribe marks

Number Correct

46-50 You are unquestionably a national authority. Write your own book.

40-45 Write a chapter for the national authority's book on antiques.

35-39 Write an article for an antiques oriented magazine.

30-34 Write a letter to a friend.

25-29 Randomly select a name from the telephone directory and write her/him a letter.

20-24 If you live alone, you are the most intelligent resident of your home.